Other books by Ben-Tzion Spitz:

Fiction:

- Joshua: Conqueror
- Destiny's Call:
Book One – Genesis
Book Two – Exodus
Book Three – Leviticus
Book Four – Numbers
Book Five -- Deuteronomy

Non-Fiction:

- Jewish Adventure in Modern China
- The Oracle and The Rabbi
- Commandments in Color (Hebrew)

Mikraot Ketanot
Torah Shorts on the Weekly Reading

מִקְרָאוֹת קְטַנּוֹת

Ben-Tzion Spitz

Valiant Publishing

Mikraot Ketanot
Torah Shorts on the Weekly Reading
Copyright © 2016 by Ben-Tzion Spitz
All rights reserved. No part of this book may be reproduced or transmitted in any form or by any means without written permission of the author.

Valiant Publishing, 333 West Merrick Road, Suite C
Valley Stream, NY 11580, USA

Author's blog: ben-tzion.com
For schools or bulk orders, contact the author directly at:
bentzispitz@gmail.com

First Edition

1 3 5 7 9 10 8 6 4 2

ISBN 978-1-937623-99-9

To Avi and Yael

Table of Contents

Introduction 1
Bereshit 3
    Sabbath of Creation 4
    "Very Good" Creation 5
    Searching for Eden 6
    Spiritual Anti-Gravity 7
Noah 8
    Perfidious Friends 9
    Acceptable Murder 10
    The Blessing of Babel 11
    Union of the Not-So-Righteous 13
Lech Lecha 14
    Super-blessed 15
    Blessings of the Wise 16
    The Source of Gravitas 17
    The Man Without Fear 18
Vayera 19
    Sacred Guests 20
    Morality Play 21
    Glorious Modesty 22
    Playing with Predestination 23
Chaye Sarah 24
    Afternoon Matchmaking 25
    To Parents of Singles 26
    Ancestral Land 27
    The Good that Evil Men Do 28
Toldot 30
    Beware the Peace Offering 31
    The Jewish Secret to Success 32
    Hunter's Deception 33
    Culinary Love 34
Vayetze 35
    Focused Prayer 36
    Mirror of Guilt 37
    Maternal Impressions 38
    Prophetic Instincts 39
    Mark Twain on the Jews 40
Vayishlach 41
    Idolatry Allergy 42
    Secret Respect 43
    Clean Prayer 44
    War Games 45
Vayeshev 46
    Deadly Gossip 47
    Work Smarter And Harder 48
    Happy Prophets 49
    Dream-makers 50
Miketz 51
    Carefully Chosen Words 52

Need-To-Know Guidance	53
Sensual Signals	54
Secrets of the Heart	55
Vayigash	**56**
Selfless Love	57
Jewish Electron Shells	58
Vegetarian Mummies	59
Sifting for Diamonds	60
Vayechi	**62**
Generational Patience	63
Second-Rate Torah Scholars	64
Joseph's Unnamed Children	65
Sabbath Soul	66
Shemot	**67**
Persistent Divinity	68
Direct Divine Doorway	69
The Cure to Hidden Pain	70
The Savior's Speech	71
Va'era	**72**
Faith is the Cure	73
The Pedigree Fallacy	74
Call of the Wild	75
Discovering God	76
Bo	**77**
Circular Assistance	78
Holy Uruguayan Dogs	79
Bargaining with God	80
Everything is Timing	81
Beshalach	**82**
Choose Your Weapon Carefully	83
Liar's Reward	84
Why Seven Days?	85
The Physics of Miracles	86
Yitro	**87**
Delayed Repercussions	88
Preparing for God	89
Hold Thy God	90
Homemade Deities	91
Mishpatim	**92**
Smooth Talkers	93
Cursing's Legacy	94
Divine Moisturizer	95
You get what you pay for…	96
Terumah	**97**
Bread of Faith	98
Portable Honor	100
Concentrated Divine Presence	101
Plain-Sight Secrets	102
Tetzaveh	**103**
Useless Superstition	104
Spiritual Ingredients	105

Rabbinic Stone Healing	106
Ripped Jeans Philosophy	107
Ki Tisa	**108**
The Labor of Thinking	109
Complete Dedication	110
Win Friends and Influence People	111
Otherworld Practice	112
Vayakhel	**113**
Wise Wives	114
Spoils of the Sabbath	115
Temple Fast-Pass	116
Vital Sermons	117
Pekudei	**118**
Blessed Intuition	119
Vayikra	**120**
The Guilt Offering	121
Selfless Self-prayer	122
Carnivorous God	123
Immortal Spirit	124
Tzav	**125**
Sinful Ignorance	126
Unholy Leftovers	127
A Life for a Life	128
Fragrant Deception	129
Shemini	**130**
Bugs in Paradise	131
Scheduling Joy	132
"Don't Lecture Me…"	133
Humans in the Zoo	134
Tazria	**135**
Animal Tension	136
A Secret of Jewish Marriage	137
Metzora	**138**
Some people never learn…	139
Holy Thumbs	140
The Sin of Haste	141
Acharei Mot	**142**
Smart Diet	143
Flawless Transmission	145
Kedoshim	**146**
Sinner's Advantage	147
Religious Convenience	148
With great power…	149
Emor	**150**
The Sin of Missed Opportunities	151
Selective Lineage	152
Repetitive Repetitions	153
The Value of the Unneeded	154
Behar	**155**
Beneficial Obedience	156
Family Reconciliation	157

Beware the Jealous	158
Bechukotai	**159**
Self-punishment	160
Bamidbar	**162**
Deathless Future	163
Overqualified	164
Lions of Israel	165
Jewish Warriors	166
Naso	**168**
Impure Prophecies	169
Nearby Exile	170
Suffering's Reward	171
Humble Hero	172
Behaalotcha	**173**
A Father's Blessing	174
The Final Battle	175
Infinite Light-givers	176
The Travel Imperative	177
Shelach	**178**
The Power of the Few	179
Coward's Failure	181
Jewish Anger Management	182
Detailed Devils, Vague Angels	183
Korach	**184**
Corruptibility	185
Too Holy	186
Destiny's Name	187
Souls in Motion	188
Chukat	**189**
Beware the Fool	190
Gentle Strength	191
Talk is Cheap	192
When "Sorry" Ain't Enough	193
Balak	**194**
Perilous Roads	195
Beware the Curse	196
Chink in our Armor	197
The Drive of Destiny	198
Pinchas	**199**
Secrets of Creation	200
Purposeful Reward	201
The Power of Honoring	202
Personal, Pure, Public	203
Matot	**204**
A Leader's Vow	205
After the Foxhole	206
Jealous and Vengeful God	207
Individuality in the Crowd	208
Masai	**209**
It's not the journey, it's the purpose	210
Devarim	**211**

Sufficient Scholars?..212
Striking While Hot...213
Home Protection...214
Vaetchanan..**216**
Anti-Demon Laser..217
Seeing is Doing...218
Give me Addiction or Give me Death...219
Ekev..**222**
Fashionable Resurrections...223
Unusual Success...224
The Illusion of Reality..225
Reeh...**227**
The Metaphysics of Charity..228
Inseparable Pair..229
Divine Entrapment..230
Prophetic Frauds...231
Shoftim..**232**
Lions of Judah...233
Monarchical Vacillation...235
"Don't do me any favors"...236
Every Man A City..237
Ki Tetze...**238**
Ugly Language..239
Foolish Friends..240
Foundations for Life..241
Individual Torah...242
Ki Tavo...**243**
Respect the Silence..244
Cosmetic Beauty...245
Secret Sins..246
Soul Hijackers...247
Nitzavim...**249**
Instant Global Cure...250
Personal and Group Judgment..251
"That could never happen to me"..252
The Worst Curse...253
Vayelech..**254**
Afterlife Conversations..255
Instant Repentance...256
Haazinu..**258**
Forging the Eternal Inheritance..259
Beware the Four Horsemen...261
Hearing-Aid for the Dead..262
Vezot Habracha..**263**
Pre-Incarnated Unity...264
Stolen Inheritance...265
Long Live the Constitution..266
International House of Prayer...267
In Memoriam - Rav Yehuda Amital ZT"L..**269**
Thanks!..**270**
About the Author..**271**

Introduction

There is a Rabbinic tradition to review the weekly Torah reading (parasha) twice every week, alongside a translation. To add to my personal education, I decided to also study alongside the parasha one of the classic commentators. After some time doing this I realized that despite my earnest reading of the texts, I couldn't remember anything afterwards!

That's when I decided to write down one nugget from the parasha every week; one insight that caught my attention. Once I was already writing, I decided via the magic of email to share these short insights with family and friends.

What commenced as a small list has grown into an email list thousands strong, in two languages, numerous writing projects, several books, a blog that has been visited by people from over 100 countries, getting Semicha (Rabbinic Ordination) and a job as the Chief Rabbi of a small South American country.

Let this be a warning to those who share words of Torah – you never know where it will lead you!

As of this writing, I'm actually into my eighth year of writing what I have called **Torah Shorts**. The commentator I started with was Sforno, followed by Hizkuni, Kli Yakar, Ohr Hachayim, Ibn Ezra, Netziv, Baal Haturim and this year I'm working on the Sfat Emet.

For this book I've chosen to include four of them: Baal Haturim, Netziv, Ibn Ezra and Ohr Hachayim. The perceptive reader will note that I've presented these in reverse order than the order in which I originally studied and wrote them. This was done on purpose, as in this book I've presented them in reverse chronological order (for me anyway), mostly to make the editing and layout somewhat easier.

Stylistically, I found a writing style that has found great success with a growing readership. I try to come out with a catchy title. I follow it with a quote from a secular source. I then provide some personal perspective before getting to the singular point from the classical commentator that originally caught my attention. I end with some hopeful or upbeat wish and after wishing all a Shabbat Shalom I end with a dedication as seemed appropriate to me that week.

Most often, the dedications refer to some event of the week, so in order to provide greater clarification for those who care for such detail, I wrote Ohr Hachayim in the Hebrew year 5772 (2011-2012), Ibn Ezra in 5773 (2012-2013), Netziv in 5774 (2013-2014) and Baal Haturim in 5775 (2014-2015). The events are of a personal nature, communal interest or global news. It may be fascinating for some readers to try to relate the dedications outside of their timing context, or as a study of my weekly preoccupations.

One thing that is lost in moving these essays from electrons to paper was that at times I made use of hyperlinks to connect readers to more information about specific people or subjects of interest. To those sensing I'm referring to something that might interest them (I realize it's hard to tell when you can't see the word underlined and in a different color, but nonetheless), you can find the original articles with their links on my blog at: ben-tzion.com

After having written these short pieces, I find I revert to them for the scheduled week to either use in one of my sermons or just to have a short *dvar torah* ready. It has served me quite well, and my hope is that it will serve you as well and be a source of insight, inspiration and connection with our Torah and some of its great commentators.

Shabbat Shalom!

Ben-Tzion Spitz בן-ציון שפיץ
Montevideo, Uruguay

Tevet 5776
December 2015

בראשית

Bereshit

[Genesis Chapters I-VI]

BERESHIT SHEMOT VAYIKRA BAMIDBAR DEVARIM   Baal Haturim
Bereshit Noah Lech Lecha Vayera Chaye Sarah Toldot Vayetze Vayishlach Vayeshev Miketz Vayigash Vayechi

Sabbath of Creation

What is without periods of rest will not endure. -Ovid

The Zohar, the prime tome of Kaballah provides dozens of interpretations for the very first word and phrase of the Bible. Many of the interpretations involve wordplay, numerology and other tools of the esoteric world, combined with mystic philosophy, often building on Talmudic sources.

Many of the concepts presented seek to understand why the universe was created, what are the guiding principles, how man came into being and for what purpose.

The Baal Haturim on the very first line, Genesis 1:1 quotes several of these ideas. One of them is that the world was created because of the Sabbath.

Stating that the world was created because of a certain idea or concept places that concept in a central, fundamental role in our existence. The Sabbath is fundamental. Not only was the world created because of the Sabbath, but if we were to imagine a world without a Sabbath, we could imagine a world quickly disintegrating into chaos and anarchy. A world of non-stop work. A world lacking human contact and relationships. A world where families lose their cohesion and communities fall apart. A world filled with materialism and starved of spirituality. A world where we become pleasure-seeking and fulfilling automatons, not resting to consider who we are or why we are here. To live a life unexamined.

Next week, the global Jewish community has called on all of our people to celebrate and experience one Sabbath together. There is an ancient rabbinic statement that if the entire people of Israel were to observe one Sabbath, the redemption would immediately come.

It's that close.

Dedication

To Chief Rabbi Warren Goldstein of South Africa for his inspired initiative of The Shabbos Project and for the professional implementation of this historic effort.

BERESHIT SHEMOT VAYIKRA BAMIDBAR DEVARIM **Netziv**
Bereshit Noah Lech Lecha Vayera Chaye Sarah Toldot Vayetze Vayishlach Vayeshev Miketz Vayigash Vayechi

"Very Good" Creation

"Teamwork is so important that it is virtually impossible for you to reach the heights of your capabilities or make the money that you want without becoming very good at it." -Brian Tracy

In a perfect world, one might wonder why God didn't create us in a much more self-sufficient fashion. Why are we so dependent on others? Why are we always in need of the help of professionals, workers, and a slew of specialized and non-specialized people in order to accomplish almost anything in our daily lives?

Is this some lack in the divine design? Was this an oversight in God's master plan? Rabbi Naftali Zvi Yehuda Berlin, also known as the Netziv, (1816-1893), implies that this dependency is exactly what God wanted.

In Genesis 1:31 God oversees the whole of his creation efforts at the end of the sixth day. He states that it is "very good." The Netziv explains that each individual component of creation was "good." However, it is the combination of all the different elements which complement each other that makes creation "very good."

May we always be there to contribute our particular capabilities to creation and may we gladly accept the assistance of others when we need it.

Dedication

To all the people who continue to assist us – it makes for a "very good" existence.

BERESHIT SHEMOT VAYIKRA BAMIDBAR DEVARIM   Ibn Ezra
Bereshit Noah Lech Lecha Vayera Chaye Sarah Toldot Vayetze Vayishlach Vayeshev Miketz Vayigash Vayechi

Searching for Eden

"Where the apple reddens never pry — lest we lose our Edens, Eve and I." -Robert Browning

Ever since Man's banishment from the Garden of Eden, we have sought to rediscover the lost paradise. Scientists, scholars and archeologists have proposed a number of locations for the historic Eden, yet none have been able to confirm (how would they do so?) where the ancient home of Adam and Eve is.

One of the more popular suggestions places the Garden of Eden near modern-day Kuwait, between the Euphrates and Tigris rivers, the only easily identifiable rivers listed in the creation story. Others have placed it in Turkey between the headwaters of those two rivers.

One of my favorite suggestions is that Israel is the site of the Garden of Eden, based on satellite imaging of pre-flood riverbeds that emanate from the Great Rift we're sitting on.

The Ibn Ezra however, provides an unusual clue as to where he thinks the Garden of Eden was situated. He states that it was on the equator, where days and nights are equivalent throughout the year. This corresponds exactly with one of the most abundant sites for ancient human fossils, Lake Turkana in Kenya, which is situated on the equator and has been termed by anthropologists "the cradle of humanity."

However, perhaps more important then finding the ancient fossils of the Garden of Eden, would be to create our own living, existential paradise on earth.

Dedication

In memory of Dr. Irvin Kaplan of Baltimore, MD. A man that healed for over four decades in Baltimore and inspired all who knew him.

BERESHIT SHEMOT VAYIKRA BAMIDBAR DEVARIM Ohr Hachayim
Bereshit Noah Lech Lecha Vayera Chaye Sarah Toldot Vayetze Vayishlach Vayeshev Miketz Vayigash Vayechi

Spiritual Anti-Gravity

"One word frees us of all the weight and pain of life; that word is love." Sophocles

My brother Boaz is a compact, slim, yet physically fit guy. For many years now, at family weddings he has taken to having my larger and more massive father sit on his shoulders. The contrast of masses always amazes me. After carrying my father for many minutes, Boaz will say, "He was light." My father will similarly echo, "I was thinking light."

Is it possible for ones feelings or emotions to somehow affect the inexorable pull of gravity? The Ohr Hachayim seems to imply so.

The Ohr Hachayim explains that in the process of creation, God could have chosen from an infinite number of geometric arrangements. He chose a sphere that orbits the sun and turns on its own axis daily. The Ohr Hachayim explains that every being therefore starts off spiritually and physically equidistant from God (who is really everywhere, though he is most often identified with the Heavens). There is no advantage to country or time zone. Every thing (the Ohr Hachayim includes mineral, vegetable and animal as well) pines for God to the limit of their capacity, from around the globe.

The pull of gravity, the equal (more or less) force that it exerts on all upon the planet is, according to the Ohr Hachayim, also a spiritual force. Our thoughts, emotional and spiritual condition can have an impact on this universal power. It is apparent that when a person is depressed, they feel heavier, while a happier person will be lighter on their feet. It may not only be psychological, there may be some physiological aspects as well (any physicists out there want to do a study?).

May we be able to lighten our spirits and our weight during this Festival of Joy.

Dedication

To my father and my brother, who will be with us this Shabbat. A gravity-defying duo.

Noah

[Genesis Chapters VI-XI]

BERESHIT SHEMOT VAYIKRA BAMIDBAR DEVARIM   Baal Haturim
Bereshit **Noah** Lech Lecha Vayera Chaye Sarah Toldot Vayetze Vayishlach Vayeshev Miketz Vayigash Vayechi

Perfidious Friends

When being dishonest, people can still tell the truth. Be mindful of the treacherous that do not lie. -Eric Parslow

The generation that God decided to destroy by flooding the land was considered particularly evil. The Baal Haturim on Genesis 6:11 gives an example of their behavior: Ruben would ask his friend Simon to guard his money as well as a persimmon. Helpful Simon, wanting to take good care of Ruben's belongings would dig up the hiding place of his own treasure and place Ruben's money and persimmon together with his own hard-earned possessions.

Later that night, Ruben would explore the grounds around helpful Simon's property. Ruben would then detect the faint but unmistakable smell of the persimmon. Ruben, with his handy shovel, proceeds to dig out his money as well as all of helpful Simon's treasure.

Now Ruben did not do anything that was "illegal". There is nothing wrong with asking his friend to guard his belongings. There is nothing wrong with going around digging in public property. If by digging one should incidentally discover something of value, strictly speaking, it is ownerless and free for the taking. There isn't even anything "illegal" with arranging things to work out that way.

However, what is patently clear is that Ruben abused and took advantage of his friend's kindness in a most horrible way. He might have done it legally; he might have never told a lie, or gone against any laws – but it is clearly, horribly wrong.

God looks beyond the letter of the law. God doesn't give us credit if we follow the laws perfectly but we corrupt the spirit. God wants the heart. God wants the soul. There is an innate morality and good that is beyond what is written in any book and He wants that as well.

May we have occasions to understand and reach the spirit of the law.

Dedication

To all the volunteers, contributors, organizers and participants in the Uruguay Shabbos Project. It is already a huge success and I look forward to together enjoying the fruit of our labors. Yasher Koach!

BERESHIT SHEMOT VAYIKRA BAMIDBAR DEVARIM Netziv
Bereshit **Noah** Lech Lecha Vayera Chaye Sarah Toldot Vayetze Vayishlach Vayeshev Miketz Vayigash Vayechi

Acceptable Murder

"Murderers are not monsters, they're men. And that's the most frightening thing about them." -Alice Sebold

There is a debate as to the moral difference between using so-called weapons of mass destruction versus old fashioned conventional weapons. They both kill; they both leave their victims equally lifeless in painful, violent, gruesome ways.

Some argue as to the hypocrisy of protesting chemical weapons, while remaining silent as to the use of bullets, machine guns, tanks, mortars, artillery, rocket-launched grenades and missiles of various shapes, sizes, payloads and flesh-tearing capabilities. I will not get into the political or economic motivations as to why some conflicts get more attention.

The Netziv on Genesis 9:5 however, does make a clear differentiation not so much as to the type of weapons of death, but rather as to the roles of the participants in a theatre of war. According to the Netziv, to kill a non-combatant is murder, no matter how they are killed, and should be punishable to the full extent. To kill a combatant is not murder and does not carry any penalty or even guilt. The Netziv goes so far as to state that even leaders sending young men into a non-existentially critical war, where they know they will lose soldiers, are not held to blame.

The question therefore is less about the weapons being used but rather who they are being used on. Murder is murder no matter how it is committed. Soldiers on the other hand, have always known that from the moment they put on their uniforms they may become casualties of war – not murder victims.

May God protect our soldiers wherever they are, and keep non-combatants away from murdering zealots.

Dedication

To Nadine Segall and Diego Turn on their upcoming wedding. I'm honored they've asked me to conduct the ceremony.

BERESHIT SHEMOT VAYIKRA BAMIDBAR DEVARIM   Ibn Ezra
Bereshit **Noah** Lech Lecha Vayera Chaye Sarah Toldot Vayetze Vayishlach Vayeshev Miketz Vayigash Vayechi

The Blessing of Babel
"There are incalculable resources in the human spirit, once it has been set free." –Hubert Humphrey

After the cataclysm of The Flood, the descendants of Noah congregated in the plains of Shinar within the Fertile Crescent, and built a city. A city with a tower that reached for the heavens. It was meant to be a city for all mankind, where all of humanity could be united in peace and harmony in one place. God however, had other plans. He confused the languages of the idealistic builders which led to the dispersion of mankind across the face of the Earth. The structure became known as the Tower of Babel and it was never completed.

Most Rabbinic commentators view the effort of the Tower of Babel as one of hubris, of man reaching to compete with God, to supplant God. They view the dispersion as a punishment. Ibn Ezra has a different take.

Ibn Ezra (on Genesis 11:3) feels that there was no sin in the construction of the Tower and neither was there a punishment. Man in his youthful idealism sought to unite all people. To unite them around a physical structure that could be perceived by all. To keep the people concentrated in one place. Not to have divisions, or borders, or geographic differences, or national allegiances. They wished for a utopian unity of all people. There was no sin in these goals – they just weren't what God planned for mankind – certainly not at that stage of history.

God wanted Man to cover the Earth, to reach for the peaks of Everest and the plains of the Serengeti, to spread and divide, to form tribal and national identities, to have unique sub-groupings of families and peoples, to diversify and differentiate. God did not want a world of people with the same language, thoughts, opinions and tastes. He wanted a pageant of ideas, a cacophony of voices, a symphony of traditions. The dispersion of the Tower of Babel was not a punishment. It was a blessing.

It has given us a world full of color, and sound, and discovery, and delight, in almost every corner of the globe. Imagine how much poorer we'd all be, if we were still congregated in some megalopolis, looking up at a tower in the plains of southern Iraq?

Thank God He kicked us out of there.

Dedication
To my brand new nephew, Azriel Zechariah Tocker, to his parents Ilan and Rachel, to his grandparents and to his four older brothers. Mazal Tov!

BERESHIT SHEMOT VAYIKRA BAMIDBAR DEVARIM *Ibn Ezra*
Bereshit **Noah** Lech Lecha Vayera Chaye Sarah Toldot Vayetze Vayishlach Vayeshev Miketz Vayigash Vayechi

To his Honor, Judge Menachem Lieberman on his promotion to Lieutenant Colonel (Sgan Aluf) of the IDF. May he keep executing justice, strongly and fairly.

BERESHIT SHEMOT VAYIKRA BAMIDBAR DEVARIM *Ohr Hachayim*
Bereshit **Noah** Lech Lecha Vayera Chaye Sarah Toldot Vayetze Vayishlach Vayeshev Miketz Vayigash Vayechi

Union of the Not-So-Righteous

Noah, through his righteousness, was able to save himself and his immediate family from world destruction. His righteousness was not enough however, to prevent the global catastrophe or to save anyone else.

The Ohr Hachayim (Genesis 6:14) draws a distinction between someone who is completely righteous (I'm not sure what that means) and someone who is not on that level (let's call them semi-righteous). The difference is apparent only in numbers.

The Ohr Hachayim claims that a union of semi-righteous people (at least ten) is superior to the lone fully righteous person. The mathematics is demonstrated further on in Genesis during Abraham's negotiations with God over the fate of Sodom and its sister cities. According to the Ohr Hachayim a union of semi-righteous is powerful enough to not only save themselves, but to save an entire city or even the entire world. It is even enough to prevent God from 'letting loose' with His wrath and wrecking havoc and destruction upon the guilty.

Hence, it is clearly superior to unite with our semi-righteous or not-so-righteous brothers than to remain alone in our "full" righteousness. The creation of a small "community" that cares one for the other, that reaches out and is concerned for others trumps the lonely saint.

May we always find those willing to unite with us, though we don't necessarily live up to saintly standards.

Dedication

To Rabbi Rami Avigdor and his Centro Kehila community-building efforts in Spanish-speaking countries.

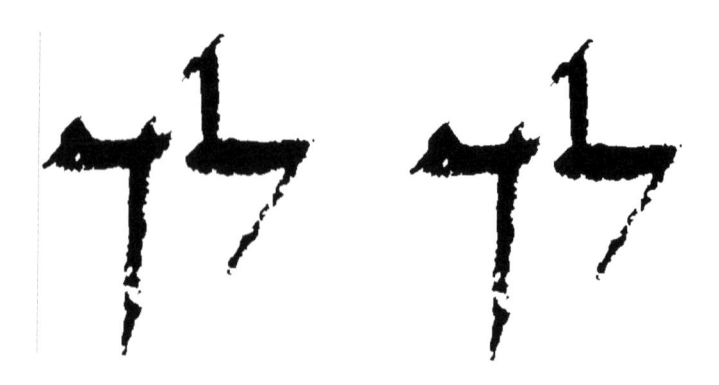

Lech Lecha

[Genesis Chapters XII – XVII]

BERESHIT SHEMOT VAYIKRA BAMIDBAR DEVARIM   Baal Haturim
Bereshit Noah **Lech Lecha** Vayera Chaye Sarah Toldot Vayetze Vayishlach Vayeshev Miketz Vayigash Vayechi

Super-blessed

Count your blessings. Once you realize how valuable you are and how much you have going for you, the smiles will return, the sun will break out, the music will play, and you will finally be able to move forward the life that God intended for you with grace, strength, courage, and confidence. -Og Mandino

After the failures of Adam, Noah and successive generations we are finally introduced to the first Patriarch, the founder of our nation, Abraham.

He was an outstanding personality. He rose to a higher calling against all opinion, pressure and odds. In return for his loyalty, his courage, his goodness and his example, God blesses Abraham.

The Baal Haturim on Genesis 12:2 enumerates seven blessings with which Abraham was graced:

1. Abraham will become a Nation
2. Abraham will receive great wealth.
3. Abraham will receive a new name (Abram was switched to Abraham)
4. Abraham himself will be considered a blessing.
5. Whoever will bless Abraham, God will ensure that they in turn are also blessed.
6. Enemies will be cursed.
7. All families of the world will be blessed by Abraham.

May we live up to the example of Abraham and also participate in his blessings.

Dedication

To Gabriel Boruchovas for going over and above the call of duty in making sure the Uruguayan Shabbos Project was a major success.

BERESHIT SHEMOT VAYIKRA BAMIDBAR DEVARIM **Netziv**
Bereshit Noah **Lech Lecha** Vayera Chaye Sarah Toldot Vayetze Vayishlach Vayeshev Miketz Vayigash Vayechi

Blessings of the Wise

"Kings may be judges of the earth, but wise men are the judges of kings." -Ibn Gabirol

I was a schoolboy in Caracas, Venezuela, when I met Rabbi Ovadia Yosef, then Chief Rabbi of Israel. In my young mind I understood he was a walking Torah scroll. I had seen some Torah scrolls previously. They contained our ancient written tradition. They were sacred. We revered them. Here was a human version, with arms and legs, eyes, ears, a mouth that poured forth words of Torah and a powerful, encyclopedic mind that contained and spread forth an ocean's worth of Torah.

Something must have touched me on that day that I should still carry such memories three and half decades later.

God tells Abraham that he will be a blessing to others. The Netziv, on Genesis 12:2, explains that the blessings of Abraham were particularly effective and powerful. He was sought out by princes and kings for his council and blessing. The Netziv relates this to the Talmudic dictum that when one is sick, they should seek out the "Chacham" (sage/wise one). Not only should one seek the potent blessings of the "Chacham", but perhaps more significantly, one should follow their advice.

May we have the good fortune of connecting with wise, blessed people.

Dedication

In memory of Harav Ovadia Yosef. The people of Israel have lost a great sage.

BERESHIT SHEMOT VAYIKRA BAMIDBAR DEVARIM   *Ibn Ezra*
Bereshit Noah **Lech Lecha** Vayera Chaye Sarah Toldot Vayetze Vayishlach Vayeshev Miketz Vayigash Vayechi

The Source of Gravitas

"If a man happens to find himself, he has a mansion which he can inhabit with dignity all the days of his life."-James A. Michener

Gravitas, Pietas, Dignitas and Virtus are the classic Roman virtues whose Latin names have survived to English and many other languages since. Both gravitas and dignitas underscore the fact that the more serious or successful a person becomes, the weightier they become (and I don't mean pounds-wise, though there is certainly a literary connection).

Ibn Ezra (to Genesis 13:2) brings our attention to the antecedent to that concept from the Hebrew language and specifically from the story of Abraham.

*"And Abram went up out of Egypt, he, and his wife, and all that he had, and Lot with him, into the South. And Abram was very **heavy** in cattle, in silver, and in gold." Genesis 13:1-2*

Ibn Ezra explains that to be weighed down with money, with livestock, etc. leads to honor. According to him, the term for honor (kavod in Hebrew) is derived from the word heavy (kaved). Likewise, the opposite of honor, disgrace (kalon) stems from the word light (kal).

So when someone calls another a lightweight, small fry, inconsequential, you now know that it stems from the Hebrew terms of light and disgraced. Likewise, heavy-hitters, big shots, heavy-duty (kaved) are all deserving of honor (kavod), because of their personal gravitas.

May we only be drawn by the gravitational pull of worthy heavyweights.

Dedication

On the birth of my newest niece, Chana, to Dr. Elisha and JJ Kahen.
To Tamara on her big birthday.

BERESHIT SHEMOT VAYIKRA BAMIDBAR DEVARIM   **Ohr Hachayim**
Bereshit Noah **Lech Lecha** Vayera Chaye Sarah Toldot Vayetze Vayishlach Vayeshev Miketz Vayigash Vayechi

The Man Without Fear

"You are as young as your faith, as old as your doubt; as young as your self-confidence, as old as your fear; as young as your hope, as old as your despair."
– General Douglas MacArthur

The Wise Men of Marvel Comics, in their marketing wisdom, subtitled their superhero Daredevil, "The Man Without Fear." Now Daredevil was not particularly powerful. He couldn't fly. He didn't have super-strength, was as fragile as any other mortal and had no special powers. His only unusual ability was that he had an internal radar/sonar that let him know what was going on around him. This was particularly useful to him, as besides not having conventional superpowers, Daredevil was also legally blind.

Despite his limited super-abilities, the character of Daredevil was truly fearless. He tackled armies of goons, the biggest crime-lords in the city, and of course powerful super-villains. All he was armed with was his billy-club, his radar-sense, his fighting and athletic prowess and his faith.

The Ohr Hachayim talks about another man with no fear. Our Patriarch Abraham. Armed with just his faith in God, Abraham leaves his home, his country, his people and ventures forth to an unknown destination. According to the Ohr Hachayim (Genesis 12:3), it was this faith, this fearlessness, that made Abraham blessed.

Not only was Abraham blessed, but he was perhaps the most blessed of all mortals. His blessing would be eternally powerful. Those who bless him and his spiritual descendants are in turn blessed, and the descendants likewise carry this power to bless. It only depends on one thing. Faith. And to achieve that faith, we need to let go of fear.

May we achieve faith, fearlessness and blessing and follow some of the footsteps of Abraham (or Daredevil).

Dedication

To some of the fearless women in my life:

To Tamara, for her fearless and successful recruiting mission to England (she is now the Assistant Director of Midreshet Tzvia – some of you may also recognize her inspiration in this week's story).

To my mother, for yet another move to a strange new land – Geneva!

To my grandmother, for a quick recovery from her hospitalization – please pray for Zahava bat Sa'ada Tichye.

Vayera

[Genesis Chapters XVIII-XXII]

BERESHIT SHEMOT VAYIKRA BAMIDBAR DEVARIM — Baal Haturim
Bereshit Noah Lech Lecha **Vayera** *Chaye Sarah Toldot Vayetze Vayishlach Vayeshev Miketz Vayigash Vayechi*

Sacred Guests

A guest never forgets the host who had treated him kindly. -Homer

In some ancient cultures, guests held a sacred and honored role. Once a person entered the tent or home of a host, they were under the host's protection and cared for in every way.

We see this quite dramatically with Abraham's wayward nephew, Lot. Lot, apparently attracted to the avarice of the Sodomites, settles his family next to the infamous city. However, he learned at least one thing from Abraham: Hospitality.

When the two disguised angels arrive in Sodom, Lot rushes to greet them and basically forces them to come as guests to his house.

The Baal Haturim on Genesis 18:5 explains that Lot was actually pained when he did not have guests and that the opportunity to host someone gave him great joy.

We see afterwards that Lot takes his hosting responsibility to such an extreme that he is willing to allow his own daughters to be harmed by a mob rather than permit anyone to touch his guests.

I don't know if we need go to such lengths to make our guests feel comfortable, but there is something special in the bond that is created when people break bread together.

May we have occasion to enjoy both hosting and being hosted by members of our communities.

Dedication

To Adrian Weiszman for spearheading the initiative of organized regular Shabbat meal hosting in our community. For more information contact proyectoshabatuy@gmail.com

BERESHIT SHEMOT VAYIKRA BAMIDBAR DEVARIM   Netziv
Bereshit Noah Lech Lecha **Vayera** Chaye Sarah Toldot Vayetze Vayishlach Vayeshev Miketz
Vayigash Vayechi

Morality Play

"Let us with caution indulge the supposition that morality can be maintained without religion. Reason and experience both forbid us to expect that national morality can prevail in exclusion of religious principle." -George Washington

Abraham arrives at Grar, land of the Philistines with his beautiful wife, Sarah. In order to protect himself from lustful, violent men ready to kill a husband so as to claim the wife, Abraham and Sarah assume the guise of siblings. Avimelech, King of Grar, claims Sarah for himself. God intervenes, warns Avimelech in a dream, Sarah is returned to Avraham and all continue with their interesting lives.

Avimelech however confronts Abraham and asks him why they lied about their identity. Abraham responds that he didn't see "fear of God" amongst the Philistines. (Recap of beginning of Genesis Chapter 20).

The Netziv on Genesis 20:11 states something surprising. He claims that the Philistines were actually a civilized, moral people and would not under normal circumstances capture a married woman or resort to murder that they may claim her. However, Abraham sensed that their morality was relativistic and not absolute. That it came from social convention and not from belief nor subjecting oneself to divine command.

Because of this "natural" morality, Abraham knew that the Philistines would have a much harder time resisting temptation. He knew that they would rationalize the permissibility of killing Abraham in order to get Sarah. That's what he was afraid of: a "morality" without God's directive. Man-made morality has been and always will be suspect.

May we live up to and attach ourselves to the ethics that we've inherited from the days of Abraham.

Dedication

To Rabbi Shmuel Eliyahu and Danny Sanderson – two very different people who inspired me this week. (See "Adventures" blog post for more details)

BERESHIT SHEMOT VAYIKRA BAMIDBAR DEVARIM   Ibn Ezra
Bereshit Noah Lech Lecha **Vayera** Chaye Sarah Toldot Vayetze Vayishlach Vayeshev Miketz Vayigash Vayechi

Glorious Modesty

"Modesty forbids what the law does not." -Seneca

Our Matriarch Sarah is considered to have been one of the most beautiful women to have ever lived. Her beauty was so extraordinary, that even into her eighties monarchs sought to possess her. Her husband Abraham, fearful of being assassinated on account of his wife, by men that would covet her, came up with the subterfuge of pretending she was his sister. This did forestall any murderous intentions, but let the kings claim her with limited trouble.

God intervenes directly, protects Sarah from the paws of amorous rulers, and arranges for Sarah to be returned to Abraham untouched. Avimelech, the King of Grar (the second monarch, after Pharaoh of Egypt, to go through the frustration of claiming Sarah, only to have to give her back to Abraham), bestows a gift upon Sarah ("ksut einayim"), translated as "a covering for the eyes." There are multiple interpretations of what this means.

The Ibn Ezra (to Genesis 20:27) explains that it was some unique type of headdress, which on one hand covered Sarah more, so that it would be harder for men to gaze upon her beauty, but on the other hand was a sign of prestige, signaling to others that she was a noble woman.

Ibn Ezra further theorizes that Avimelech's extraordinary gift included something (it's not clear to me if it's an object, a protective force of slaves, a law and/or a press release) that allowed Sarah to drop the pretense of being Abraham's sister, and made public the fact that they are married and that she is not to be pursued. Now, Abraham's existence and presence as her husband would be Sarah's defense against inappropriate interest in her.

I'll refrain from any further wishes or comments, as the last time I wrote on this subject, I got some heated responses. Everyone draw their own conclusions.

Dedication

To Shoshi Taragin and Gidon Kupietzky on their engagement. Mazal Tov to them and their families!

To Scientific American Magazine. They reported about a study that reinforces what Jewish law has implied for a very long time: Platonic relationships are mostly a one-sided phenomena.

BERESHIT SHEMOT VAYIKRA BAMIDBAR DEVARIM   *Ohr Hachayim*
Bereshit Noah Lech Lecha **Vayera** Chaye Sarah Toldot Vayetze Vayishlach Vayeshev Miketz Vayigash Vayechi

Playing with Predestination

"Our character…is an omen of our destiny, and the more integrity we have and keep, the simpler and nobler that destiny is likely to be."
-George Santayana (1863 – 1952)

The people of ancient Sodom were reportedly a highly unsavory crew. God, despite Abraham's pleas, decides to literally wipe the city off the map. One man and his family however, are destined to be saved. Lot, nephew of Abraham, is the only half-decent man in the entire metropolis. His wife and two unmarried daughters are absconded out of the city by an angelic task force.

However, according to the Ohr Hachayim (Genesis 19:1) Lot was not necessarily deserving of the destined salvation. He claims that the first purpose of the angels' visit to Sodom was to create a merit, a reason, a justification for Lot to be rescued from the impending doom. Lot does achieve that merit, by graciously hosting the visiting angels. By offering his hospitality in an inhospitable city, by showing kindness where cruelty surrounded him, Lot earned deliverance. If Lot had not lived up to this Abrahamic heritage, he would not have survived Sodom. However, God first had to give Lot the opportunity, the chance to perform this good, even heroic deed in order to save himself.

Lot grabbed the chance God gave him with both hands and thereby merited salvation and the destiny in store for him. He had no way of knowing, of course, that his hospitality was a direct cause of the predestined rescue.

Destiny does await us and opportunities to achieve it surround us. May we realize the chances God gives us to do good, in order to reap the rewards.

Dedication

To all the Alyn bikers, for their predestined and amazing completion of the ride. You are inspiring.

חיי שרה

Chaye Sarah

[Genesis Chapters XXIII-XXV]

BERESHIT SHEMOT VAYIKRA BAMIDBAR DEVARIM   Baal Haturim
Bereshit Noah Lech Lecha Vayera **Chaye Sarah** Toldot Vayetze Vayishlach Vayeshev Miketz Vayigash Vayechi

Afternoon Matchmaking

Like everything which is not the involuntary result of fleeting emotion but the creation of time and will, any marriage, happy or unhappy, is infinitely more interesting than any romance, however passionate. -W. H. Auden

The shortest, though perhaps the most challenging prayer of the day is the afternoon prayer (Mincha). The morning one (Shacharit) is the longest, but for those who introduce it into their routine, it turns into an excellent start to their day. The night prayer (Arvit) is not too long and is a great way to cap off ones busy day. But Mincha is different. It involves a very conscious decision to stop what one is in the middle of, and set aside some minutes for God.

The Baal Haturim on 24:63 reminds us of the tradition that our patriarch Isaac was the one who instituted the Mincha prayer. What is interesting about the Biblical source for this tradition is that immediately after praying that afternoon, Isaac's bride-to-be appears.

Was it Isaac's selfless time for God that earned him the appearance of a wife? Does stopping our personal pursuits and beseeching God for intervention in our lives actually lead to some stronger divine involvement?

The Baal Haturim ends his explanation with the famous dictum, Matza Isha Matza Tov (One who found a wife, found goodness). This perhaps goes against a growing trend that glorifies singlehood.

May those who seek a spouse merit divine intervention and those who have a spouse remember and reinforce the goodness that marriage is meant to be.

Dedication

To the single people in our lives. May they find the right partner – at the right time.

BERESHIT SHEMOT VAYIKRA BAMIDBAR DEVARIM Netziv
Bereshit Noah Lech Lecha Vayera **Chaye Sarah** Toldot Vayetze Vayishlach Vayeshev Miketz Vayigash Vayechi

To Parents of Singles

"The joys of parents are secret, and so are their grieves and fears." - Francis Bacon

There is a unique, special joy that a parent feels upon the successful marriage of their child. Likewise, there is a unique, special pain a parent feels when a child fails to connect with their life's mate.

There is much debate, discussion and controversy as to the extent a parent should be involved in encouraging and facilitating the marriage of their child, if at all. Obviously much will depend on the individual personalities, family dynamics, relationships and more. Some parents are known to harass their children about the topic to the point of seriously damaging the child-parent relationship. Some parents shy away from the topic as if it were some divine command to steer clear of even hinting at the issue, but then leave the child without any guidance or support. Most fall somewhere in between, doing their best to walk the tightrope of feelings, emotions, hopes, expectations and disappointments that life throws our way.

When it is time for our Patriarch Isaac to marry, we find his father Abraham completely in the driver's seat. Abraham gives the direction, provides the priorities, the funding, all the resources and assistance he can bring to bear, to ensure that his son marries well. The entire episode is curiously prefaced by the statement that Abraham was old. The Netziv on Genesis 24:1 explains that the details of Abraham's age are to clarify for us the reason Abraham himself did not personally go to seek Isaac's bride. If he would have been younger and of stronger health, the Netziv says, Abraham would have had the obligation to personally travel to Haran to see to and ensure the matching of Isaac with Rebecca.

The Netziv makes it clear that a parent is obligated to do all they can, all that is within their means and capacity, (with diplomacy and sensitivity), to encourage, support and enable the marriage of their children.

May we dance at many weddings together.

Dedication

In memory of my grandmother Zahava Rosenthal, on the first Yarzheit since she left us. One of her special gifts and joys was to match couples together.

BERESHIT SHEMOT VAYIKRA BAMIDBAR DEVARIM   Ibn Ezra
Bereshit Noah Lech Lecha Vayera **Chaye Sarah** *Toldot Vayetze Vayishlach Vayeshev Miketz Vayigash Vayechi*

Ancestral Land

"Each blade of grass has its spot on earth whence it draws its life, its strength; and so is man rooted to the land from which he draws his faith together with his life." -Joseph Conrad

Our Matriarch Sarah dies and Abraham spends a veritable fortune to buy a plot to bury his wife. The Torah goes into painstaking detail as to the negotiations, the back and forth, the language each party used and the final sale price (400 shekel, the equivalent back then to buying a high-rise apartment building in Hong Kong).

It is curious the amount of time the text spends on Abraham's purchase of land in Israel, his determination to buy the land at all costs and his refusal to accept it as a gift. The Ibn Ezra (on Genesis 23:19) suggests an answer.

He offers that there is something special, something unique about the land of Israel. He explains that out of all of the land on the planet, out of all of the countries in the world, Israel is the best place to be buried. It is the ideal resting place for the dead.

He adds one other comment. It is also the best place for the living.

Dedication

In memory of my grandmother, Mrs. Zahava Rosenthal, who died last week in New York and was buried in her ancestral plot, in Haifa, Israel. Attached are links to the eulogy I gave (original Hebrew or English translation).

BERESHIT SHEMOT VAYIKRA BAMIDBAR DEVARIM   Ohr Hachayim
Bereshit Noah Lech Lecha Vayera **Chaye Sarah** Toldot Vayetze Vayishlach Vayeshev Miketz Vayigash Vayechi

The Good that Evil Men Do

"Nothing is easier than to denounce the evildoer; nothing is more difficult than to understand him." – Fyodor Dostoevsky (1821 – 1881)

As children, we like both our heroes and our villains pure. We prefer clear demarcations of good and evil. The heroes should be complete role models, with nary a fault. The villains should be bad, through and through. Even the villain's good deeds must have a conniving rationale. Reality however, is more complex.

The Bible and our lives are populated with distasteful personalities. The Rabbinic commentators over the centuries did not hold back in their criticism of these horrid people. They often received the moniker "Evil One" appended to their names.

One of the more colorful villains of the Bible is Laban the Aramite. Over time, he proved to be a niggardly, scheming, lying, greedy, egocentric, power-hungry, idol-worshipping and ungrateful, slave-driving employer and father-in-law to our Patriarch Jacob. (That makes him our great, great, great, grandfather many many times over).

The Ohr Hachayim though, squeezes a good act out of this otherwise Evil Laban. When we first meet Laban, he is introduced by the Bible:

*"And Rebecca had a brother, and his **name** was Laban." Genesis 24:29*

The Ohr Hachayim is perplexed by this introduction, for apparently there is a well known dictum in the Midrash, that for the righteous, their **"name"** comes **before** them.

Meaning, they are introduced as: "his **name** was Boaz," where the word **"name"** precedes the actual personality, while the sinners are introduced as "Naval was his **name**," with the word **"name"** coming after the villain.

So how is it that this most evil of men, the one that we denounce on Passover night for wanting to destroy all of Israel (as opposed to Pharaoh, that only wanted to kill the men) is introduced with the introduction of the righteous?

The Ohr Hachayim reads the scene of Laban's first appearance. A strange man (Abraham's servant) approaches Laban's young sister, Rebecca, gives her gifts and asks personal questions. Laban's first instinct is to protect his sister and confront this strange man. Just for this simple thought to defend his sister's honor, God introduces this otherwise highly villainous ancestor of ours, as if he were righteous.

May we always find good in the evil around us.

BERESHIT SHEMOT VAYIKRA BAMIDBAR DEVARIM *Ohr Hachayim*
Bereshit Noah Lech Lecha Vayera **Chaye Sarah** Toldot Vayetze Vayishlach Vayeshev Miketz Vayigash Vayechi

Dedication

To the various inept and corrupt politicians in the world (I'm not sure which is worse). Though we often (rightfully) disparage them, we are thankful for their moments of goodness.

תולדות

Toldot

[Genesis Chapter XXV-XXVIII]

BERESHIT SHEMOT VAYIKRA BAMIDBAR DEVARIM   Baal Haturim
Bereshit Noah Lech Lecha Vayera Chaye Sarah **Toldot** Vayetze Vayishlach Vayeshev Miketz
Vayigash Vayechi

Beware the Peace Offering

Peace, in international affairs, is a period of cheating between two periods of fighting. -Ambrose Bierce

Because of a famine in the mountains of Canaan, our patriarch Isaac heads to the area of Gerar by the Mediterranean coast. There he gets entangled in a variety of problems with the Philistines in general and their King Avimelech in particular. Isaac has the concern, which echoes the experiences of his father Abraham, that the locals may kill him in order to claim his beautiful wife, Rebecca.

Isaac and Rebecca, following the previous generation's example, pretend to be brother and sister. However, Avimelech discovers the truth and chastises Isaac for the deception. Thereafter, we see that Isaac is blessed with tremendous economic success despite Philistines sabotaging his wells and Avimelech eventually banishing him from Gerar.

Isaac settles by Beer Sheva in the Negev and continues to flourish. King Avimelech, accompanied by his General Fichol, visit Isaac seeking peace with him. Both Isaac and the Baal Haturim on Genesis 26:29 are suspicious of the sudden amity on the part of Avimelech.

The Baal Haturim explains that Avimelech truly wanted to kill Isaac and only after repeated failed efforts does Avimelech pause and tries the strategy of seeking peace – it would seem more out of fear of Isaac's growing power than for any benevolence or caring for Isaac. It was purely short-term self-interest. The Philistines would remain mortal enemies for centuries to come.

May we achieve peace despite the efforts of our enemies.

Dedication

To our soldier Eitan on the completion of his training and his assignment.

BERESHIT SHEMOT VAYIKRA BAMIDBAR DEVARIM   Netziv
Bereshit Noah Lech Lecha Vayera Chaye Sarah **Toldot** Vayetze Vayishlach Vayeshev Miketz Vayigash Vayechi

The Jewish Secret to Success

"Education is an ornament in prosperity and a refuge in adversity." – Aristotle

There are undoubtedly few nations in the history of the world that have invested more in the education of its people than the Jewish nation. Jewish education is by most accounts the reason for our extraordinary survival and success despite millennia of discrimination and persecution.

It is therefore both sad and ironic that in recent decades, after all this time, the Jewish people (as a whole) have either watered-down or completely abandoned their connection to Jewish texts and tradition. It is even more ironic to consider that those very same texts that we treasured, fought for, and even died for, are now being sought after and taught by others in countries like South Korea to gentile populations, where Talmud is apparently a growing interest.

The Torah recounts how our forefather Isaac encounters wild economic success during his sojourn in the land of Canaan. The Netziv on Genesis 26:5 explains that Isaac's success was a direct result of his education, following in the footsteps and guidance of his father Abraham. The Netziv learns from Isaac's example that study and practice of Torah, of Jewish law and tradition, leads to business success.

Let's open up those books and connect to the source of true success.

Dedication

To all of my students in my various Torah classes. It is an honor and a privilege to teach you and I am enriched by it.

BERESHIT SHEMOT VAYIKRA BAMIDBAR DEVARIM Ibn Ezra

Bereshit Noah Lech Lecha Vayera Chaye Sarah **Toldot** Vayetze Vayishlach Vayeshev Miketz Vayigash Vayechi

Hunter's Deception

To hunt skillfully, one must master deception. To lay a hidden trap, to conceal an ambush, to wait until the right moment to strike, all require subterfuge and the art of tricking ones victim into believing the situation is safe, secure, calm, when in fact it is imminently deadly.

The Bible, in introducing the sons of Isaac – Esau and Jacob, tells us that Esau was a hunter. Ibn Ezra (on Genesis 25:27) explains that it is coming to highlight Esau's deceptive nature. For Esau it was easy to lie, to lure prey into his clutches, to disguise himself, to blend into the foliage when necessary. He had the capacity to attack at a moment's notice, to kill his quarry. The Rabbis from the very outset deride such predatory characteristics.

As a contrast, Jacob is depicted as a mild, scholarly, tent-dwelling shepherd, not cut out for the hunt, for deception, for subterfuge. It is therefore the ultimate irony that Esau is tricked out of his ostensibly deserved blessing by his otherwise honest brother.

That sincere Jacob disguised himself, pretended to be Esau, lied to their father and thereby robbed the blessing from Esau the deceiver, could only have been utterly humiliating to a skilled hunter such as Esau.

Deceivers and hunters, watch out. The honest ones are the most dangerous.

Dedication

To the Israeli leadership and security forces that hunted and killed one of the more damaging enemies of Israel. May they continue to do so.

BERESHIT SHEMOT VAYIKRA BAMIDBAR DEVARIM   *Ohr Hachayim*
Bereshit Noah Lech Lecha Vayera Chaye Sarah **Toldot** Vayetze Vayishlach Vayeshev Miketz Vayigash Vayechi

Culinary Love

You may not have realized it, but we are descendants of chefs. Our ancestors had a love of food and its preparation. While ancient man may have constantly been preoccupied with the preparation of their next meal, it seems our Patriarchs were particularly passionate about the taste and quality of their repast.

The Rabbis state that Esau was a regular provider of food to his father Isaac, hence the request that Esau provide a special meal so that Isaac may bless him. There is also the famous scene of Jacob preparing a meal and Esau, his brother, trading his Firstborn status for some "red soup."

The Ohr Hachayim (Genesis 25:29) explains that Jacob had been preparing the meal for Isaac, their father. Jacob saw that Esau's meals for his father developed a special bond between Isaac and Esau, and Jacob may have sought to replicate such an effect.

They would agree that a way to a man's heart certainly passes through his stomach.

May we appreciate all the chefs in our lives and grow closer through the joy of meals together.

Dedication

To our wonderful hosts and friends for a fantastic celebratory dinner.

Vayetze

[Genesis Chapters XXVIII-XXXII]

BERESHIT SHEMOT VAYIKRA BAMIDBAR DEVARIM   Baal Haturim
Bereshit Noah Lech Lecha Vayera Chaye Sarah Toldot **Vayetze** Vayishlach Vayeshev Miketz Vayigash Vayechi

Focused Prayer

No steam or gas ever drives anything until it is confined. No Niagara is ever turned into light and power until it is tunneled. No life ever grows until it is focused, dedicated, disciplined. -Harry Emerson Fosdick

In the first and perhaps most famous of the Biblical dreams, Jacob sees a ladder that reaches the heavens with angels ascending and descending. The scene has been recreated in art and literature, has been interpreted widely and has served as a metaphor for connecting heaven and earth.

The Baal Haturim on Genesis 28:12 explains that the sound of the righteous praying constructs a ladder for angels to ascend. He further states that we have it in our power to also create heavenly ladders. All we need to do is focus during our prayers. Our focusing completes the ladder. If we are focused during our prayer then he assures us that our prayers will indeed ascend on these spiritual ladders and reach their destination.

And another source as to the benefits of praying:

The influence of prayer on the human mind and body is as demonstrable as that of secreting glands. Its results can be measured in terms of increased physical buoyancy, greater intellectual vigor, moral stamina, and a deeper understanding of the realities underlying human relationships. -Dr. Alex Carrel

May we make the time to pray and when we do so, may we have the ability to focus.

Dedication

Mazal Tov to Nadia and Daniel Kacowicz on their wedding. May their focused prayers come true!

BERESHIT SHEMOT VAYIKRA BAMIDBAR DEVARIM   Netziv
Bereshit Noah Lech Lecha Vayera Chaye Sarah Toldot **Vayetze** Vayishlach Vayeshev Miketz Vayigash Vayechi

Mirror of Guilt
"The vices we scoff at in others, laugh at us within ourselves." -Thomas Edward Brown

Jacob works for his greedy, deceptive father-in-law, Lavan, for twenty years. Jacob is the perfect worker. He cares for and guards Lavan's livestock with incredible attention and responsibility. Lavan becomes a wealthy, powerful man due to Jacob's hard work. Jacob has a spotless record. Not one of the animals are hurt, attacked or stolen during Jacob's long years of service. It was an unheard of achievement of diligence, self-sacrifice and productivity. He didn't take any sick days or vacation and he worked the night shift as well. It's not clear when he slept. Jacob was probably the employee of the century.

It is therefore highly surprising that when Jacob and family, under God's orders, escape from Lavan, Lavan chases them and accuses Jacob of no less than robbery.

How can Lavan suspect his star employee, the man who built his empire, of petty theft? The Netziv on Genesis 31:41 explains that Lavan is exhibiting a common human trait. Lavan is accusing a completely blameless person of a trait that he himself possesses. The Netziv states that it is normal for people who possess a certain characteristic to assume other people have the same one. A thief will assume that others are thieves as well.

Therefore, when one person accuses or degrades someone else of some failing, we don't need to look too far as to why the accuser would be familiar with such failings.

May we be careful of who we accuse and what we accuse them of. It may reveal more than what would be desirable.

Dedication
To the Rabbi Yisrael Meir Kagan (1838-1933) also known as the Chofetz Chaim, for his groundbreaking book of the same name on the Jewish laws of watching what we say.

BERESHIT SHEMOT VAYIKRA BAMIDBAR DEVARIM   Ibn Ezra
Bereshit Noah Lech Lecha Vayera Chaye Sarah Toldot **Vayetze** Vayishlach Vayeshev Miketz Vayigash Vayechi

Maternal Impressions

"The mother's heart is the child's schoolroom." -Henry Ward Beecher

I recall, when we were expecting our first child, there was a popular trend of playing classical music for the embryo. The belief was that it somehow affected the unborn child, helped with its development and would make it smarter. My wife ignored the fad and listened to music she liked, which may explain why all of our children are such good dancers.

When our Patriarch Jacob wanted to affect the coloring of the livestock under his care, in order to increase the payout that his father-in-law/employer Laban was supposed to give him, Jacob strategically placed white sticks at the watering hole for the fertile animals to see.

Ibn Ezra (on Genesis 30:39) explains that what a mother sees during her pregnancy will have an affect on what the child will look like. Hence, by Jacob placing the white sticks in front of the animals, he was able to have an impact on how the new livestock turned out.

May we always gaze upon good, beautiful and healthy sights, which will hopefully have a positive affect on us and our children.

Dedication

To the Iron Dome defense system. The sight of it knocking Hamas missiles out of the sky was beautiful to behold.

BERESHIT SHEMOT VAYIKRA BAMIDBAR DEVARIM Ohr Hachayim
Bereshit Noah Lech Lecha Vayera Chaye Sarah Toldot **Vayetze** Vayishlach Vayeshev Miketz Vayigash Vayechi

Prophetic Instincts

"The ultimate function of prophecy is not to tell the future, but to make it." – Joel A. Barker

Jews are notorious for significant accomplishments across a breadth of fields and disciplines. There have been multiple theories as to the outsized proportion of Jewish Noble Prize winners and other intellectual, medical, technological, political, artistic and economic achievements.

Some have explained it is the extreme Jewish value of education (the only culture to have close to 100% literacy throughout history). Others like to refer to the unique Talmudic system of thinking and analysis (now being emulated in some ways in the Far East). I have my own theory: Prophecy. And the Ohr Hachayim backs me up.

I don't mean prophecy in the narrow sense of God speaking to an emissary or carrying God's message or predicting the future. I mean something more subtle.

On his journey out of Canaan, the Patriarch Jacob has a now-famous dream. He dreams of a ladder, with its legs on the earth reaching to the heavens. He sees angelic beings ascending and descending these supernatural steps. The Ohr Hachayim (Genesis 28:14) explains that the vision of the ladder was an extremely powerful symbol – a symbol with deep meaning to Jacob's descendents.

The heavenly ladder symbolizes our connection to God. It symbolizes our ability to connect with Him. To reach him, one rung at a time; though we may be firmly rooted on earth, with can still grasp the divine. The Ohr Hachayim makes another statement. He says the ladder is a sign to all Jacob's descendants that they too can reach Prophecy. They can hear God whispering to them. They can feel that divine insight in their stomachs that drives them to excel. They can listen to the supernatural instincts that lead them to accomplishments beyond expectations. That is the prophetic instinct I'm talking about.

May we listen to God's whispers – we may need some quiet to do so.

Dedication

To Mark Twain. I can't help thinking about his essay on Jews when I wave the flag of tribal pride. I've included it below. It's always nice to review.

BERESHIT SHEMOT VAYIKRA BAMIDBAR DEVARIM   *Ohr Hachayim*
Bereshit Noah Lech Lecha Vayera Chaye Sarah Toldot **Vayetze** Vayishlach Vayeshev Miketz
Vayigash Vayechi

Mark Twain on the Jews

If the statistics are right, the Jews constitute but one quarter of one percent of the human race. It suggests a nebulous puff of star dust lost in the blaze of the Milky Way. Properly, the Jew ought hardly to be heard of, but he is heard of, has always been heard of. He is as prominent on the planet as any other people, and his importance is extravagantly out of proportion to the smallness of his bulk.

His contributions to the world's list of great names in literature, science, art, music, finance, medicine and abstruse learning are also very out of proportion to the weakness of his numbers. He has made a marvelous fight in this world in all ages; and has done it with his hands tied behind him. He could be vain of himself and be excused for it. The Egyptians, the Babylonians and the Persians rose, filled the planet with sound and splendor, then faded to dream-stuff and passed away; the Greeks and Romans followed and made a vast noise, and they were gone; other people have sprung up and held their torch high for a time but it burned out, and they sit in twilight now, and have vanished.

The Jew saw them all, survived them all, and is now what he always was, exhibiting no decadence, no infirmities of age, no weakening of his parts, no slowing of his energies, no dulling of his alert but aggressive mind. All things are mortal but the Jews; all other forces pass, but he remains. What is the secret of his immortality?

–Mark Twain, September 1897

וישלח

Vayishlach

[Genesis Chapters XXXII-XXXVI]

BERESHIT SHEMOT VAYIKRA BAMIDBAR DEVARIM   Baal Haturim
Bereshit Noah Lech Lecha Vayera Chaye Sarah Toldot Vayetze **Vayishlach** Vayeshev Miketz Vayigash Vayechi

Idolatry Allergy

Whatever a man seeks, honors, or exalts more than God, this is the god of his idolatry. -William B. Ullathorne

I grew up with a variety of allergies. There were foods, substances and smells that would make me sick and specifically trigger respiratory difficulties. In my youth, during visits to a specific person's home, I would unexpectedly start to sneeze uncontrollably. I was informed afterwards that every time I would have a sneezing attack it coincided with someone smoking marijuana in a nearby room.

But perhaps the most surprising allergy of all was not to any particular molecule that made its way into my respiratory system. In the course of my teenage travels, I had opportunity to be exposed to real live examples of idol worship: people praying, chanting, bowing down and performing religious service in front of statues. Just the sight, the approach, just to be in the same physical space or structure as the good old-fashioned idolaters made me physically uncomfortable. At the time I was not yet aware of the prohibition by Jewish law of entering a Temple of idols. Nonetheless, my body, apparently of its own volition, reacted negatively to any encounter with these structures and activities, typically with feelings of nausea.

In the Torah we see a similar but broader national effect. Jacob's wayward brother Esau, together with his growing clan, leaves their ancestral land of Canaan. The Baal Haturim on Genesis 36:7 explains that because of the divine presence in Canaan, Esau could not stay there with his brother Jacob. He says that a similar effect occurred in the separation between the children of Israel and the Egyptians who needed to live in different areas. We cannot be in the same place as idolaters, and vice versa.

May we identify the idolatry in our lives and separate ourselves from it and from within us.

Dedication

To my Tikvah Fund friends. It was thrilling to explore the Bible and discover excellence.

BERESHIT SHEMOT VAYIKRA BAMIDBAR DEVARIM **Netziv**
Bereshit Noah Lech Lecha Vayera Chaye Sarah Toldot Vayetze **Vayishlach** Vayeshev Miketz Vayigash Vayechi

Secret Respect

"What is told into the ear of a man is often heard a hundred miles away." -Chinese Proverb

Jacob fears his upcoming encounter with his estranged brother Esau. Esau is on his way to meet Jacob with a force of 400 men. Jacob sends multiple delegations carrying livestock as gifts to his dangerous brother.

They finally meet in a dramatic and emotional moment with hugging, kissing and crying. Jacob then abases himself in a manner that is almost embarrassing. He calls his brother "master" repeatedly, while referring to himself as "your servant." Whether Jacob was sincere or not in his abnegation is open to debate, but what the Netziv on Genesis 32:5 makes clear is that Jacob was thorough and consistent in assuming the servile role.

The Netziv points out that not only is Jacob subservient in front of Esau, but also when he is out of sight he shows his brother the same level of respect. In Jacob's private discussions with his own servants, he likewise refers to his brother as "my Master" and to himself as "his servant." The Netziv signals that we should cultivate the habit of referring to people with their proper names, titles and with respect, both in public and in private. Others will pick up on how we speak and use the names and terms we use, for better or worse.

May we speak properly of others and in respectful terms.

Dedication

To Rabbi Ariel Kleiner. A man for whom I have great respect, despite ideological differences.

BERESHIT SHEMOT VAYIKRA BAMIDBAR DEVARIM   Ibn Ezra
Bereshit Noah Lech Lecha Vayera Chaye Sarah Toldot Vayetze **Vayishlach** Vayeshev Miketz Vayigash Vayechi

Clean Prayer

"Cut your morning devotions into your personal grooming. You would not go out to work with a dirty face. Why start the day with the face of your soul unwashed?" -Robert A. Cook

Through fate and circumstance, I've had opportunity to observe many types of groups and religions at prayer in different parts of the world. Whether it was Christians in one of the resplendent churches of the city of Ouro Preto, Brazil, Muslims in the Blue Mosque of Istanbul or Buddhists in Bangkok, there are a number of common denominators to the act of prayer.

There is typically a seriousness, an awe, a somberness, in the realization that one is confronting a higher power. It is perhaps ironic then that in Judaism, especially in a number of Orthodox Jewish synagogues, these aspects may be lacking in communal prayer. One is more likely to find disinterest, boredom, chatting and a great rush to be done with it. It would appear as more of an obligation that one needs to discharge rather than an opportunity to reach God in a place, at a time and with a group that is particularly structured for such a purpose.

Perhaps it is the burden of having such meetings so frequently. Perhaps it is the regularity of it. The predictability. The liturgy. I don't know. However, perhaps the worst offense is when someone rushes into the synagogue with dirty clothing.

After the fracas of Jacob's children with the Canaanite city of Shechem, Jacob orders his camp to get rid of any idols, wash up and change their clothing. Ibn Ezra (on Genesis 35:2) adds that this is the source that when one goes to a fixed place to pray, he should do so with a clean body and garments.

May we always show the appropriate attitude when praying, inside and out.

Dedication

To my friends and neighbors in synagogue. Let's cut the chatter a bit.

BERESHIT SHEMOT VAYIKRA BAMIDBAR DEVARIM   *Ohr Hachayim*

Bereshit Noah Lech Lecha Vayera Chaye Sarah Toldot Vayetze **Vayishlach** Vayeshev Miketz Vayigash Vayechi

War Games

"Skillfullness in moving an opponent about comes through
Positioning the opponent is compelled to follow
And gifts the opponent is compelled to take.
Through the promise of gain,
An opponent is moved about
While the army lies in wait."
– Sun-Tzu

In the confrontation between Jacob and his brother Esau, Jacob is classically depicted as the weaker party. Esau approaches with 400 warriors against Jacob's shepherd family. Jacob debases himself in front of the formidable Esau who in the end is merciful and lets Jacob continue on his way.

But based on the Ohr Hachayim, I see Jacob as a master strategist that was ready to pounce on Esau if the war-like brother decided to attack.

I was always confused by the explanation that Jacob split his camp into two, so that one of the camps might "flee" if the other was attacked. The Ohr Hachayim (Genesis 32:8) explains that the second camp wasn't prepared to flee, but rather to attack. The first camp was a "front," a peaceful guise to keep matters calm.

If Esau could keep the peace, that was preferable, but if not, Jacob was ready for war. He was ready, but not hopeless or even desperate as we might have imagined. Jacob performs a dangerous covert overnight mission of the night-crossing of the Yabok River. He places his forces at the location of his choosing. He leads Esau's force with his "gifts" to his preferred location. He meets Esau with a "peaceful" camp, while a fully armed and ready force is waiting in the wings for Jacob's signal.

We don't know what might have been if the brothers would have conducted open warfare. I would have put money on Jacob (with God's assistance) having the superior tactical advantage and besting his brother Esau.

May we be spared the harms of war, but be prepared to fight when we must.

Dedication
To my son, Eitan, on signing up with the IDF this month.

וישב

Vayeshev

[Genesis XXXVII-XL]

BERESHIT SHEMOT VAYIKRA BAMIDBAR DEVARIM — Baal Haturim
Bereshit Noah Lech Lecha Vayera Chaye Sarah Toldot Vayetze Vayishlach **Vayeshev** Miketz Vayigash Vayechi

Deadly Gossip

Fire and swords are slow engines of destruction, compared to the tongue of a Gossip. -Sir Richard Steele

In my current role, many people seek my intervention in a variety of personal issues. Usually they tell me details of matters that personally affect them. However, once in a while, they will start to gossip. That is when I respectfully, but firmly, ask them to stop gossiping.

On one particular occasion, I asked the speaker to stop and I quoted to him the Talmudic dictum that the Baal Haturim on Genesis 37:2 references: Gossip kills three different people. It kills the one who speaks it, it kills the one who is spoken about and it kills the one who is listening. A week later one of those three was killed in a tragic accident.

The Talmud further states that gossip is worse than murder, adultery and idolatry combined. I finally understood that it is more than exaggerated rhetoric. The three cardinal sins break the bonds of life, of marriage and of faith respectively. Gossip breaks all of these and more. It breaks the bonds of friendship and of community that are just as vital, if not more so than life, marriage and faith. I have seen this happen. I have seen the consequences of gossip. I have seen the destroyed lives.

So let's control ourselves. Let's think before we share that juicy bit of gossip. It is deadly – and you never know who will be the next fatal victim.

Dedication

To all those who restrain themselves from gossiping. And to all those completing the 3-year study cycle of Maimonides' Mishne Torah. The new cycle starts this Sunday. Join us!

BERESHIT SHEMOT VAYIKRA BAMIDBAR DEVARIM Netziv
Bereshit Noah Lech Lecha Vayera Chaye Sarah Toldot Vayetze Vayishlach **Vayeshev** *Miketz Vayigash Vayechi*

Work Smarter And Harder

"Talent is cheaper than table salt. What separates the talented individual from the successful one is a lot of hard work." -Stephen King

I don't recall when I first heard the American truism of "Work Smarter NOT Harder." It was a consultant's motto. A manager's lodestone. Brains, not brawn. Let's think of solutions for the lazy man. Let's design time and effort-saving devices in order to work less. Work became a dirty word. Success would come from intelligence. Manual labor was worse than being unemployed.

Now there are millions of debt-ridden hyper-educated unemployed and millions of job openings for those willing to use their hands and backs.

Success may require a return to manual and hard labor. However, the Netziv on Genesis 39:6 has a different source for employment success.

The text tells us that when Joseph is a slave in Egypt, his masters notice his divine success. Did Joseph have a sign over his head proclaiming God's assistance? Did God sign his name on Joseph's work in flashing neon lights? What does it mean that they realized his success came from God?

The Netziv explains that it became obvious to Joseph's masters that his success was out of all proportion to his capabilities or efforts. The only answer was that it came from God. Not that we don't need talent, intelligence or hard work – but often God is the final ingredient for success.

May we experience success in all our good work.

Dedication

To Mike Rowe who has elevated my interest and appreciation for "Dirty" Jobs.

BERESHIT SHEMOT VAYIKRA BAMIDBAR DEVARIM Ibn Ezra
Bereshit Noah Lech Lecha Vayera Chaye Sarah Toldot Vayetze Vayishlach **Vayeshev** Miketz Vayigash Vayechi

Happy Prophets

"An ounce of cheerfulness is worth a pound of sadness to serve God with." -Thomas Fuller

Jacob's sons convince their father that his favorite son Joseph is dead. Jacob falls into an inconsolable grief. Ibn Ezra (on Genesis 37:35) adds that Isaac, Jacob's father, shared in the grief for his missing grandson and that both Isaac and Jacob were no longer able to commune with God because of their sorrow.

Ibn Ezra learns about sadness cutting the ability to communicate with God from the story of the prophet Elisha. Elisha the Prophet (see II Kings) had been sad ever since his master, the prophet Elijah, had passed away. Elisha called for a minstrel to play a tune to cheer him up, which then allowed him to talk to God.

Similarly, as long as Jacob and Isaac were sad, they would be unable to receive any prophetic messages. Hence the dictum that one cannot effectively contact God if one is in a poor frame of mind.

May we always strive for happiness and thereby more readily reach God.

Dedication

To the Comedy for Koby comedians who just completed their 2012 Israel Tour. May they continue to bring good cheer wherever they go.

BERESHIT SHEMOT VAYIKRA BAMIDBAR DEVARIM Ohr Hachayim
Bereshit Noah Lech Lecha Vayera Chaye Sarah Toldot Vayetze Vayishlach **Vayeshev** Miketz
Vayigash Vayechi

Dream-makers

"So many of our dreams at first seem impossible, then they seem improbable, and then, when we summon the will, they soon become inevitable."

– Christopher Reeve

Joseph had a power. He had a power to interpret the strange, irrational, often incomprehensible images of the unconscious mind that we call dreams. He was able to read the prophetic messages conveyed in the dreams and alert the waking world.

The Ohr Hachayim (Genesis 40:8) thinks that we have the cause and effect of dreams mixed up. He claims that the interpretation of the dream is what makes it come real. The dream is just the canvas of future potential. The interpretation, the enunciating, the giving of form and structure and content to the visions of the mind, brings the dream to the real world and gives it shape, purpose and fulfillment.

He adds one caveat. The dream must be interpreted that day. It cannot be allowed to linger as a mist in the mind. It must be seized, jumped upon, brought to the light of day and out of the shadows of the night. Only then do we have a hope of the dreams becoming real. Only by acting on those dreams can we hope to see them fulfilled.

No one understood or realized how Joseph's power worked. No one understood that Joseph was creating reality as he desired from the stuff of dreams. No one realized that if they were determined enough they could make their dreams come true. Now we know.

May we have worthy dreams, and when we wake up in the morning, let's verbalize them and make them happen.

Dedication

To Thedor Herzl. He was not the first to have the dream. The dream was beating in the heart of the Jewish nation for two thousand years. He interpreted the dream. He wrote about the dream. He brought the dream to our brothers throughout the Diaspora and helped make it real.

מקץ

Miketz

[Genesis Chapters XLI-XLIV]

BERESHIT SHEMOT VAYIKRA BAMIDBAR DEVARIM   Baal Haturim
Bereshit Noah Lech Lecha Vayera Chaye Sarah Toldot Vayetze Vayishlach Vayeshev **Miketz**
Vayigash Vayechi

Carefully Chosen Words
We would often be sorry if our wishes were granted. -Aesop

Jacob's sons had been to Egypt and back, where they had been strangely received and then rebuffed by their brother Joseph whom they didn't recognize. Joseph, Viceroy of Egypt, had given them vital food during the worldwide famine, imprisoned one brother, Simon, and warned them that they would not be received again without the youngest brother, Benjamin.

Back in Canaan, Jacob prohibits his sons from returning to Egypt with his beloved Benjamin. In a rash display of confidence, the eldest son, Reuben, states to his father: let me take Benjamin with us and if I do not return him, you can kill my two children. Jacob does not respond to this incomprehensible statement.

Rabbinic commentators take Reuben to task for such a deadly statement. The Baal Haturim on Genesis 42:37 takes the rebuke a step further and claims that Reuben's declaration actually did lead to the tragic death of two of his descendants. His notorious descendants, Datan and Aviram, lead a rebellion against Moses in the desert and are miraculously swallowed up by the earth as divine punished. While they were clearly deserving of death, the Baal Haturim directly relates their fate to the unfortunate choice of words by their ancestor.

Let's be very careful with the words and expressions we use – God is always listening, and even if it is in jest, or even if we don't mean it – He might decide to make it come true.

Dedication
To the memory of Nissan ben Shlomo (Neil Israel), father of our dear friend Rachel Zlatkin.

BERESHIT SHEMOT VAYIKRA BAMIDBAR DEVARIM   Netziv
Bereshit Noah Lech Lecha Vayera Chaye Sarah Toldot Vayetze Vayishlach Vayeshev *Miketz*
Vayigash Vayechi

Need-To-Know Guidance
"Knowledge comes by eyes always open and working hands; and there is no knowledge that is not power." -Ralph Waldo Emerson

In our age of information overload, there is certain knowledge that at times we are the only ones that are privy to it. It is usually in the personal realm. A friend shares a secret. A family member tells us news first. At other times it is not necessarily information conveyed, but an insight that is reached. You finally understand why a coworker behaves a certain way. You notice your neighbor acting differently. You witness something that no one else paid attention to.

The theological question is why are we the ones to possess this unique knowledge and what are we to do with it?

Pharaoh dreams a dream that prophesies the fate of the Egyptian empire. The Netziv on Genesis 41:39 explains that God provides unique information specifically to those that can and should do something about it. Pharaoh needed to be given the vision of Egypt's future because he was the only one who had the power and the responsibility to act upon that information.

When we are given exclusive information, it is because we need to know and we need to act. Sometimes the act may be to keep quiet, but show some empathy. Sometimes it may be to give a helping hand in a discreet way. Sometimes it may be to rouse the entire world to a cause.

May we use our special insights in the proper fashion.

Dedication
To the German Ambassador to Uruguay, Dr. Heinz Peters, for his embassy's unique, quiet but generous support of the Jewish community's Holocaust Remembrance Library.

BERESHIT SHEMOT VAYIKRA BAMIDBAR DEVARIM   Ibn Ezra
Bereshit Noah Lech Lecha Vayera Chaye Sarah Toldot Vayetze Vayishlach Vayeshev **Miketz** Vayigash Vayechi

Sensual Signals

"If real is what you can feel, smell, taste and see, then 'real' is simply electrical signals interpreted by your brain." – Morpheus, The Matrix

Do you ever taste sound? Hear a view? Smell a touch? See a scent? It would seem physically impossible; however it is part of our language. We talk about sweet sounds, loud lights and various other confusions of the senses.

However, there are some people for whom mixtures of senses are common. There is a condition known as Synesthesia whereby people will actually see different colors, hear different sounds, feel different textures, smell different scents and/or taste different flavors, when no such stimulus is present.

Our Patriarch Jacob speaks with a cross-sensory metaphor when he "sees the food in Egypt" while he's sitting in Canaan listening to the reports of the food in Egypt. Ibn Ezra (on Genesis 42:1) picks up on the language and provides the first description of Synesthesia centuries before modern medicine diagnosed the condition.

Ibn Ezra explains that because all the sensory inputs connect and are interpreted by the brain, sometimes they get mixed up, hence the beautiful, artistic and surprising cross-sensory metaphors that we end up with.

May we keep mixing metaphors to our listeners' sharp consternation or bright delight.

Dedication

To synesthete physicist Richard Feynman. Other notable synesthetes include Billy Joel, Itzhak Perlman and Nikola Tesla.

BERESHIT SHEMOT VAYIKRA BAMIDBAR DEVARIM   *Ohr Hachayim*
Bereshit Noah Lech Lecha Vayera Chaye Sarah Toldot Vayetze Vayishlach Vayeshev **Miketz** Vayigash Vayechi

Secrets of the Heart
"The heart has its reasons which reason knows nothing of." – Blaise Pascal (1623 – 1662)

Chemistry between people is an unusual phenomenon. How or why certain people get along and others don't is a mystery that has confounded scientists and matchmakers since the beginning of time. Some may explain the confluence of interests, backgrounds, priorities, tastes, intelligence and a long checklist of factoids that will determine the success of human interaction, whether it be friends, relatives or spouses.

Predictors of compatibility are often right, but just as often wrong. Two people who otherwise seem entirely attuned, for some reason cannot stay in the same room with each other. Or two people who have almost nothing in common become life-long friends.

The Ohr Hachayim (Genesis 42:8) proposes that in the interaction between two people, it is often the heart that is in driver's seat. Hearts are perceptive. They communicate with each other on a subconscious level. The Ohr Hachayim adds that hearts may tell secrets to each other. They may confirm or deny what the mind is not yet aware of, or refuses to acknowledge.

In the back-and-forth between hearts a message can percolate to the conscious mind. "I like him," the heart will say. Or "he's a jerk," the heart will confirm. Or "that's my long lost brother," as with Joseph and his siblings.

May our hearts tell us no lies and may they always interact well with the hearts around us.

Dedication
To my friends of the heart. Though we may have little in common, the heart knows otherwise.

ויגש

Vayigash

[Genesis Chapters XLIV-XLVII]

BERESHIT *SHEMOT VAYIKRA BAMIDBAR DEVARIM*   Baal Haturim
Bereshit Noah Lech Lecha Vayera Chaye Sarah Toldot Vayetze Vayishlach Vayeshev Miketz
Vayigash Vayechi

Selfless Love

We never know the love of the parent till we become parents ourselves. - Henry Ward Beecher

It seems, the Patriarch Jacob knew that if he descended to Egypt from the land of Canaan, it would be a one-way trip. He would not be able to return to the Promised Land in life. He probably also knew that it would signal the beginning of the prophesied exile and enslavement of his descendants.

However, the moment he discovers that his beloved and missing son Joseph is alive and well in Egypt, Jacob doesn't hesitate and immediately goes to reunite with his long-lost son.

The Baal Haturim on Genesis 44:29 compares the love and self-sacrifice of Jacob to the natural instinct a mother has for her child. A cow that resists going to the slaughterer because it senses impeding death will rush to the same place if it hears the cry of its calf. So too the maternal instinct is to ignore whatever danger stands in the way of reaching ones child.

May we have and feel the sentiments of love – without the danger.

Dedication
To new and experienced mothers alike.

BERESHIT SHEMOT VAYIKRA BAMIDBAR DEVARIM   Netziv
Bereshit Noah Lech Lecha Vayera Chaye Sarah Toldot Vayetze Vayishlach Vayeshev Miketz Vayigash Vayechi

Jewish Electron Shells

"The ordinary scientific man is strictly a sentimentalist. He is a sentimentalist in this essential sense, that he is soaked and swept away by mere associations." -G. K. Chesterton

There is an unusual phenomenon that occurs upon the counting of the tribes of Israel. Everyone knows that there are twelve tribes; however, the identity of those tribes seems to switch depending on the occasion.

The twelve tribes are based on the twelve sons of Jacob: Reuben, Shimon, Levi, Judah, Yissachar, Zevulun, Gad, Asher, Dan, Naftali, Joseph and Benjamin. However, once the tribes of Israel leave Egypt and move to the desert, a change occurs. The tribe of Levi is taken out of the mix, presumably because of its priestly status and the tribe of Joseph is split into two, named after Joseph's sons: Menashe and Ephraim. However, there are times that Levi is counted and on those occasions Menashe and Ephraim once again collapse into the entity called Joseph.

In chemistry, we learn about electrons, their orbits, how many electrons fill a shell and how that gets atoms to form into molecules. While the identity of the particular electron can and will change, the number of electrons that complete a shell is both fixed and crucial.

The Netziv on Genesis 46:27 explains that a similar function (he doesn't refer to chemistry) is occurring upon the counting of the tribes. The number twelve is inviolate. The tribes of Israel must always number twelve. The identity or composition of each tribe is secondary. If Levi is out, then Joseph expands to Menashe and Ephraim. If Levi is in, they contract back to Joseph again, keeping the number twelve intact.

There is a similar principle in the formation of a minyan, (the quorum of ten Jewish men required for public prayer). We don't look at the caliber or importance of a particular participant – what matters, what is crucial, is that the count be full.

May we always be counted amongst noble causes and associations.

Dedication

To the family members arriving in Montevideo for the Bar-Mitzvah. We're getting closer to that minyan.

BERESHIT SHEMOT VAYIKRA BAMIDBAR DEVARIM   *Ibn Ezra*
Bereshit Noah Lech Lecha Vayera Chaye Sarah Toldot Vayetze Vayishlach Vayeshev Miketz Vayigash Vayechi

Vegetarian Mummies

"It is useless for the sheep to pass resolutions in favor of vegetarianism, while the wolf remains of a different opinion." -W. R. Inge

In more than one place the Torah recounts that it was repulsive for the Egyptians to eat with the Hebrews. Barring a specific bigotry, we see the Egyptians are otherwise happy to be ruled by Joseph and invite his brothers to positions of leadership. So why the abhorrence of eating together?

Another clue to the Egyptian distaste of the Hebrews is the fact that the Hebrews are shepherds and the Egyptians didn't want any shepherds (and presumably sheep) around. The Ibn Ezra (on Genesis 46:34) states that the Egyptian problem was simply that they were vegetarians at the time. They didn't eat any meat. They had nothing to do with meat products. They couldn't even sit at the same table with a meat-eater.

I think this helps explain a curious verse (Genesis 39:6), which describes Joseph's master, Potiphar, as happy with everything Joseph does except the "lehem" he eats. "Lehem" is conventionally translated as bread; however, it can mean any food. I think that in this case Potiphar merely disapproved of the meat included as part of Joseph's Hebrew diet.

May everyone eat good, healthy, nourishing food and not get too obsessed with the other guy's diet.

Dedication

To Hannah Filer and Greg Bank on the occasion of their marriage tonight. Mazal Tov!

BERESHIT SHEMOT VAYIKRA BAMIDBAR DEVARIM **Ohr Hachayim**
Bereshit Noah Lech Lecha Vayera Chaye Sarah Toldot Vayetze Vayishlach Vayeshev Miketz **Vayigash** Vayechi

Sifting for Diamonds

"It is no measure of health to be well adjusted to a profoundly sick society." – Jiddu Krishnamurti

We live in a confusing and confused world. We worship people for their looks, or physical prowess, or talent, or money, or power. We strive to emulate them, wearing what they wear, doing what they do, with minimal regard to the moral component of the equation. One might refer to this ongoing period of ethical darkness as "Exile".

We have been in a long Exile, but it is purposeful. The first account of extended Exile for the Children of Israel in the Bible is the account of Jacob and his sons leaving the land of Canaan to relocate in the Egyptian Empire. Egypt was the dominant culture of the time and considered by rabbinic commentators to be the moral cesspool of the world, mired in crass materialism and a worship of death that exceeded their value of life. Why would God choose this of all places to send the nascent nation of Israel?

The Ohr Hachayim (Genesis 46:3) claims that Jacob's Exile and every Exile since then serve a vital, positive purpose in the history of the world and the mission of mankind. We are purposely placed in a location that may not be ideal, that does not have the values or ideals that we have or that we believe to be correct. Often we are affected or corrupted by the darkness that envelopes us. Our purpose is to find, create and expand the light within that darkness.

The Ohr Hachayim refers to the purpose of Exile as "drawing holiness out of impurity." We cannot and are not meant to live in ivory towers. We are surrounded and embedded within a deep, pervasive foulness that clouds the mind and spirit from an early age. But it is neither hopeless nor impenetrable. As individuals and as a community our mission is to find the diamonds around us and within us and lift them from the drudge we may be in. We must then care for those diamonds, polish them and let their light shine forth.

The diamonds are our souls and that of those around us. It is the good deed, the kind word, the moral choice, the ethical decision. It is rising above material greed and instant gratification. It is choosing wisdom and education over popular culture and mindless entertainment. It is going against the current of the purveyors of filth and cruelty. It is the courage and the strength to believe in holiness in a world that laughs at the concept. That is the purpose of Exile.

May we shine in our respective Exiles and merit enjoying the subsequent Redemption.

BERESHIT SHEMOT VAYIKRA BAMIDBAR DEVARIM *Ohr Hachayim*
Bereshit Noah Lech Lecha Vayera Chaye Sarah Toldot Vayetze Vayishlach Vayeshev Miketz *Vayigash* Vayechi

Dedication
Please pray for God's intervention for Chanoch Refael ben Dvora.

Vayechi

[Genesis Chapters XLVII-L]

BERESHIT SHEMOT VAYIKRA BAMIDBAR DEVARIM Baal Haturim
Bereshit Noah Lech Lecha Vayera Chaye Sarah Toldot Vayetze Vayishlach Vayeshev Miketz Vayigash *Vayechi*

Generational Patience
There are times when God asks nothing of his children except silence, patience and tears. -C. S. Robinson

A great evil was done to Joseph. His very brothers, his very flesh and blood, plan to kill him, but then change their mind and have him sold as a slave. Years later, when they meet again and at the very moment when Joseph can have his vengeance, he instead forgives them.

Years after that, after their father Jacob passes away, his brothers are still unconvinced by Joseph's mercy. Joseph reiterates that he harbors no ill will, that he does not seek a redress for the wrongs that his brothers afflicted upon him.

However, in the last verses of the book of Genesis, the last words Joseph speaks in his life, he makes his brothers' children swear that they will return his body to the land of Israel. The Baal Haturim on Genesis 50:25 asks why Joseph didn't make this demand of his own children, who presumably have a greater responsibility to see to the wishes of their patriarch.

The Baal Haturim answers that in this instance we are finally seeing, in a very subtle way, Joseph's demand for the long-delayed justice for the sin of the brothers. The brothers were responsible for exiling Joseph from the land of Canaan, and specifically from Shechem. It is their responsibility to return him to Canaan. Joseph's remains are finally carried by Moses himself and then by Joshua, who buries him by the city from which he was taken – Shechem.

May we be spared from causing or suffering injustices, and may we have the strength and patience to bear them when they occur.

Dedication
To God, who we forget about, don't take seriously enough, or take for granted. He works out everything in the end.

BERESHIT SHEMOT VAYIKRA BAMIDBAR DEVARIM   Netziv
Bereshit Noah Lech Lecha Vayera Chaye Sarah Toldot Vayetze Vayishlach Vayeshev Miketz Vayigash **Vayechi**

Second-Rate Torah Scholars

"The honest work of yesterday has lost its social status, its social esteem." -Peter Drucker

Maimonides, in his magnum opus, the Mishne Torah, has harsh words for Torah scholars that avoid work. In his Laws of Torah Study, Chapter 3, Law 3, he states:

"Anyone who comes to the conclusion that he should involve himself in Torah study without doing work and derive his livelihood from charity, desecrates God's name, dishonors the Torah, extinguishes the light of faith, brings evil upon himself, and forfeits the life of the world to come."

The Netziv takes a softer approach. He doesn't call such individuals damned, shameful, faith-killing, evil-mongering people whose souls are destined for eternal oblivion. He just calls them second-rate.

While Reuben, Shimon and Levi are castigated in Jacob's final blessings to his sons, and Judah and Joseph receive long and beautiful partings, it is the second son of Joseph, Ephraim, who is the surprise winner in Jacob's final orations. Jacob places Ephraim in front of Menashe, his older brother. The Netziv on Genesis 49:13 says that Ephraim is placed first because of his studious and spiritual level, due to his dedication to Torah study. The Netziv differentiates between Ephraim's level which was achieved on his own steam, and that of his uncle Yissachar.

There was a famous partnership between two of Jacob's sons, Zebulun and Yissachar. Zebulun was the merchant and his descendants supported the studious descendants of Yissachar. Zebulun is always mentioned before Yissachar, as Yissachar's Torah accomplishments are only thanks to the financial backing of Zebulun. However, Ephraim stands first, on his own, deserving greater respect and honor than the dependent Yissachar.

May we stand on our own feet, whenever we can, and thereby reach greater heights.

Dedication

To my son, Netanel, on his Bar-Mitzvah. May he become a first-rate Torah scholar.

BERESHIT SHEMOT VAYIKRA BAMIDBAR DEVARIM   Ibn Ezra
Bereshit Noah Lech Lecha Vayera Chaye Sarah Toldot Vayetze Vayishlach Vayeshev Miketz Vayigash **Vayechi**

Joseph's Unnamed Children

"If you would not be forgotten as soon as you are dead, either write things worth reading or do things worth writing." -Benjamin Franklin

Did Joseph have more than two sons? The Torah only lists Ephraim and Menashe as Joseph's sons and their names are noted repeatedly and prominently throughout the Bible. Grandfather Jacob elevated their status to equal that of his own sons, thereby making them full-fledged Tribes of Israel.

But did Joseph have any other children?

Before his death, Jacob blesses Joseph and his sons with a most unusual blessing:

"And now your two sons, who were born to you in the land of Egypt before I came to you in Egypt, are mine; Ephraim and Menashe, even as Reuben and Simeon, shall be mine. **And your children that you had after them shall be yours; they shall be called after the name of their brethren in their inheritance."** *-Genesis 48:5-6*

These verses have consternated many commentators who've gone to great pains to explain what it means, as there is no other mention or names anywhere else of any other children of Joseph.

Ibn Ezra (on Genesis 48:4) in his typical no-nonsense style says that the verses are saying what they seem to be saying, namely that Joseph did have other children, but only the two older ones were elevated, and received honor and unique status within the Israelite hierarchy. The other children of Joseph (we don't even know how many others there were) were of less significance and therefore did not merit either mention or listing in the genealogical records. In the annals of the Torah, these unnamed children were subsumed into the nomenclature of their older, more famous brothers.

Is that the fate of the unnamed? To be forgotten to the point of nonexistence?

Dedication

To our unnamed soldiers and heroes. Though they may not be celebrated, someone knows and someone remembers.

To the people at heartrescuenow.com – enabling the saving of lives.

BERESHIT SHEMOT VAYIKRA BAMIDBAR DEVARIM   Ohr Hachayim
Bereshit Noah Lech Lecha Vayera Chaye Sarah Toldot Vayetze Vayishlach Vayeshev Miketz
Vayigash **Vayechi**

Sabbath Soul

"The joy of a spirit is the measure of its power." – Ninon de Lenclos (1620 – 1705)

There is a well-known kabalistic belief that on the Sabbath we receive an "additional soul." Somehow we have an added spiritual component that is supposed to heighten our appreciation and enjoyment of that special weekly day of rest.

Scientifically no one has found a way to measure or test for this extra metaphysical occupation of our bodies. The Ohr Hachayim however believes there is a very simple way to determine the presence of the Sabbath spirit.

Our Patriarch Jacob was renamed by God "Israel." However, throughout the biblical text there is a dichotomy in regularly alternating uses of both "Jacob" and "Israel." The Ohr Hachayim (Genesis 47:28) explains that "Israel" is the more ideal, fulfilled name, while "Jacob" is a more anxious or saddened name. When Jacob was affected by his sorrows and concerns he was merely "Jacob." However, when he was happiest, when he connected fully with God, an additional spirit rested on him – then he was "Israel."

The Ohr Hachayim says it is the same with the Sabbath spirit. When one prepares for the Sabbath; when one is joyous about the upcoming day of rest; when one is ready to leave material concerns and modern distractions and focus on relationships, on family, on God, on self – then an otherworldly spirit descends upon you and you are filled with light.

If you see someone smiling and content on the Sabbath, it's a sure bet they have that "additional soul."

May we understand, prepare and enjoy the Sabbath.

Dedication

To Ahad Ha'am and his famous quote: "More than the Jews have kept the Sabbath, the Sabbath has kept the Jews."

שמות

Shemot

[Exodus Chapters I-VI]

Persistent Divinity

There is genius in persistence. It conquers all opposers. It gives confidence. It annihilates obstacles. Everybody believes in a determined man. People know that when he undertakes a thing, the battle is half won, for his rule is to accomplish whatever he sets out to do. -Orison Swett Marden

God chose Abraham to found the Chosen Nation. His first son, Ishmael, from an early age already, didn't really follow his father's footsteps. God tries again with Abraham's second son, Isaac. Isaac is blessed with twins. The firstborn, Esau, while retaining good relations with his father, was not cut out to continue the path of Abraham. God continues with the second twin, Jacob. Finally, after the third generation, Jacob has twelve sons and they all continue in God's path. They are the founding tribes of the Nation of Israel.

The Baal Haturim on Exodus 1:5 compares the above chronology to an architect who builds a palace. The architect's first effort was with one pillar. The palace did not last long. He tried again with two pillars. Same result. He tries once again with three pillars with the same failure. Finally, he goes all out and designs the palace with twelve columns. The palace remains steady until this day.

May we never be discouraged by defeat or failure in our noble enterprises. Persistence is key to success, which are both divine qualities.

Dedication

To the Jewish summer communities of Las Toscas and Atlantida. We are looking forward to a special Shabbat together.

Direct Divine Doorway

"Materialism is the only form of distraction from true bliss." -Doug Horton

Moses sees the burning bush from afar. Curious, he approaches. The voice of God commands him to remove his shoes, for he is on holy ground.

The Netziv on Exodus 3:5 reads an allegory into God's first words to Moses. If you want to approach Me, if you want direct contact with Me, you need to separate from your stuff. It may be as mundane as your shoes. It may be something good and useful for everyday life and comfort. But if you want clear, uninterrupted access to Me, you need to leave the material behind. Stop thinking about your stuff. Stop dealing with your stuff. Give Me your full undivided attention and I'll be there, waiting.

The Netziv adds that it's not for everyone and it's not all the time. We cannot walk around the whole day shoeless. We cannot ignore the basic and material aspect of our lives. But you can connect directly to God when you separate yourself from the mundane, when you're in a sacred space. This doesn't negate the ability to find God in the mundane – but perhaps it is simpler and more direct.

May we be able to take ourselves away from materialism, even if for brief moments, to encounter God more fully.

Dedication

To "The Story of Stuff Project". It is a great effort of Tikun Olam (fixing the world).

The Cure to Hidden Pain

"If pain could have cured us we should long ago have been saved." - George Santayana

Something gnaws at your mind. A pain dull, yet sometimes sharp. Specific and then amorphous. Catastrophic then minor. It is a pain you hesitate to admit to yourself, let alone another human being. But it is real. It hurts. And it doesn't seem to go away.

The Jewish slaves of Egypt suffered a variety of torments; physical, mental, spiritual. They were demeaned every way possible. They cried out to God. Sometimes the cries were shrill calls of agony heard by fellow sufferers. Other times they were whimpering whispers of defeat heard by no human ears.

Ibn Ezra (on Exodus 3:7) explains that God heard both types of pain. He heard the visible, public pain, but He also saw the hidden private pain.

When God released the Jews from their bondage, He also cured them. He saved them from the direct physical torture and enslavement, but He also freed them from the spiritual anguish which they could not reveal.

God's healing touch is something we strive to recall and recapture on a daily basis. Sometimes He's the only one listening. Let's take advantage.

Dedication

To Hadass and Ehud Ilan on their wedding. Mazal Tov!

The Savior's Speech

"Be a craftsman in speech that thou mayest be strong, for the strength of one is the tongue, and speech is mightier than all fighting." -Maxims of Ptahhotep, 3400 B.C.

In the movie, "The King's Speech," there is a painfully poignant scene when the prince has to address the nation on public radio. He stutters horribly to his eternal shame. It is hard to imagine a more embarrassing scenario.

It is no wonder then, that Moses, apparently also saddled with speech impairment, begs God not to send him as His delegate to Pharaoh and the Jewish nation. God gives Moses an interesting answer:

"And the Lord said unto him: 'Who has made man's mouth? Or who makes a man dumb, or deaf, or seeing, or blind? Is it not I the Lord?" Genesis 4:11

The Ohr Hachayim posits that God is telling Moses that not only does He know that Moses has this handicap, but that it was given to Moses on purpose. And because of this handicap He wishes Moses to overcome it and become the greatest orator in Jewish tradition.

The Ohr Hachayim gives two possible endings to Moses' speech impediment. One is that thanks to God's intervention, Moses overcame the physical impediment and was able to speak clearly once he had to.

The other, perhaps more interesting possibility, is that Moses gave all of his speeches while still having some sort of speech defect. God apparently wanting to make a point: that you don't need to be perfect in every single trait in order to fulfill God's commands. Even our great teacher Moses, whose main physical function was to speak, did so with a handicap – and did it better than anybody else.

May we appreciate the health we have, and not be bitter over the God-given impairments.

Dedication

To Dr. Anthony Beukas, my speech professor at Yeshiva University. I still remember some of his lessons.

וארא

Va'era

[Exodus Chapters VI-IX]

BERESHIT **SHEMOT** VAYIKRA BAMIDBAR DEVARIM   Baal Haturim
Shemot **Va'era** *Bo Beshalach Yitro Mishpatim Terumah Tetzaveh Ki Tisa Vayakhel Pekudei*

Faith is the Cure

The salvation of this human world lies nowhere else than in the human heart, in the human power to reflect, in human meekness and human responsibility. -Vaclav Havel

The greatest, most powerful, most important orator in Jewish history, Moses, started off with some type of speech impediment. Commentators have a variety of opinions as to exactly what the problem was, but one thing that is abundantly clear is that Moses had no desire to speak publicly. He was so perturbed by his condition that he was willing to argue with God Himself to be spared from being the divine spokesman.

God berates Moses and asks him who he thinks gives man the capacity to speak in the first place? God seems particularly harsh with Moses on this count. The question is why does God give Moses such a hard time on an issue that anyone who has ever felt discomfort or even sheer terror in front of an audience can appreciate? Why was God so demanding, even insistent that this poor, speech-challenged man should have to speak in front of the mortal ruler of the most powerful empire on Earth? Couldn't God have chosen a natural orator, a seasoned politician, even a classroom teacher? Why did he have to focus on a lonely desert shepherd for whom the extent of discourse up until then was probably limited to giving directions to sheep?

According to the Baal Haturim on Exodus 6:30, Moses needed to have faith that God has the power to rectify the situation. God chose Moses on purpose, knowing his limitations and perhaps even because of his limitations. God knows that Moses can and will overcome them. He just needed to be placed in the position to have the necessity to overcome his challenges. Otherwise, he may have forever remained incapacitated. What angered God about Moses' fear and denial was his lack of faith. All that he needed to overcome was faith.

It was clearly not a simple or direct path for Moses, but eventually he acquires that faith and becomes the fundamental leader of the Jewish people.

May we each overcome our particular challenges and thereby merit to contribute in our own way to our people.

Dedication

To Ed Stelzer. It's incredible where challenges and faith can lead us and how roads diverge and then intertwine.

The Pedigree Fallacy

"The person who has nothing to brag about but their ancestors is like a potato; the best part of them is underground." -Sir Thomas Overbore

In Jewish circles, much weight is often given to a person's "Yichus" – his ancestry. If the person is descendent from a great line of Rabbis, we are instantly impressed by their prestigious lineage.

The Torah at times goes out of its way to give the genealogy of key personalities. Aaron the High Priest is introduced via his great-grandfather, Levi, followed by his grandfather, Kehat, and his father, Amram. To round out the picture, we are also told about Aaron's children and grandchild, Pinhas (a future High Priest). Aaron's is clearly *the* great priestly family of Israel with a mighty lineage.

The Netziv on Exodus 6:14 however, is not impressed by the powerful ancestry. He ironically comes to his conclusion from the mention of Aaron's much more famous brother, Moses. He explains that Moses is mentioned in the verse on his own merit – not that of his ancestors. Moses was great because of the connection he developed with God and his absorption of the divine will. Moses reached the height of human potential because of his intimate attachment to God's Torah. The Netziv takes a step further and claims that greatness in Torah is superior to any "Yichus" – to any ancestry, as holy and noble as it might be.

May we appreciate whatever great ancestors we may have – but establish our own good names.

Dedication
To the descendants of great personalities.

BERESHIT **SHEMOT** VAYIKRA BAMIDBAR DEVARIM　　　　Ibn Ezra

Shemot **Va'era** Bo Beshalach Yitro Mishpatim Terumah Tetzaveh Ki Tisa Vayakhel Pekudei

Call of the Wild

"Nature has been for me, for as long as I remember, a source of solace, inspiration, adventure, and delight; a home, a teacher, a companion." - Lorraine Anderson

Pharaoh has a slave rebellion brewing. A discredited former prince of Egypt has taken up their cause. He is imposing and impressive, and though Pharaoh suspects Moses is resorting to cheap magic tricks, there is something threatening, even frightening about the tall Hebrew leader.

Pharaoh wants a break. But he is behind schedule and over budget on his grand construction projects. The priesthood has been snickering behind his back about his poor leadership and even questioning his divinity.

All Pharaoh wants to do is get out of the palace. He wants to breathe some fresh air and cool his heels in the soothing water of the Nile.

Ibn Ezra (on Exodus 8:16) claims that it was the custom of monarchs to go out to the river every morning. It is good for the eyes, Ibn Ezra explains. Imagine how flummoxed Pharaoh must have been to be greeted by Moses on his lone foray into the tranquility of nature.

May we remember the nature that we have access to, and likewise drink in its healthy and reviving effects (without rebel leaders interrupting our sojourn).

Dedication

To the snow! We've been blessed with a good six inches of beautiful, white, fluffy, snow-ball throwing, snow-man building, pristine snow! Followed by blue skies!

BERESHIT **SHEMOT** VAYIKRA BAMIDBAR DEVARIM   Ohr Hachayim
Shemot **Va'era** Bo Beshalach Yitro Mishpatim Terumah Tetzaveh Ki Tisa Vayakhel Pekudei

Discovering God

"The beginning of knowledge is the discovery of something we do not understand."

Frank Herbert (1920 – 1986)

About four millennia ago, the world was polytheistic. There was an ingrained, widely held belief that there was a multiplicity of gods. A god of the sun, of the river, of rain, of fertility, major gods, minor gods, gods in human form, gods with animal characteristics, gods of gold, of silver, of stone, of clay. Whatever the human imagination could construct, the human spirit could believe in.

In preparation for redeeming the Hebrew nation from the bondage of Egypt, God names each of the Patriarchs, Abraham, Isaac and Jacob, in His announcement to Moses. The Ohr Hachayim (Exodus 6:3) states that it was in the merit of each of these great founders of the Israelite line that the Jewish nation was released from slavery. The Ohr Hachayim explains what the greatness of each Patriarch was. In explaining the greatness of Abraham, he claims that it was for one reason alone: Abraham's discovery of God.

The Ohr Hachayim declares that it's no big deal to believe in God when you are taught so from childhood. To have the belief in God as part of your upbringing, culture and social reality is good and proper, but doesn't compare to the challenge of someone who had to figure it out for themselves. Someone who can look at a pagan world, at a world consumed by materialism, self-worship and the worship of strange gods (movie stars, athletes, money, etc.) and can still find and reveal the divine in this world is worthy of redemption for himself, his progeny and those around him.

May we rediscover God every day.

Dedication

To the first blessing of the Silent Prayer, where *we* actually *bless* God, the God of our Patriarchs, the Shield of Abraham.

בא

Bo

[Exodus Chapters X-XIII]

Circular Assistance

In helping others, we shall help ourselves, for whatever good we give out completes the circle and comes back to us. -Flora Edwards

According to the Midrash (old post-biblical accounts and stories of biblical events and personalities), Jethro, future father-in-law of Moses, was one of Pharaoh's counselors. The Midrash states that Jethro argued for the benevolent treatment of the Jews at the time when Pharaoh ordered the drowning of all male babies. When Jethro saw his advice ignored and noticed the growing anti-Jewish climate, he escapes from Egypt and resettles in neighboring Midian.

Years later, Moses flees Egypt, after Pharaoh seeks to kill him for the murder of an Egyptian. Moses ends up in Midian, meets Jethro's daughters and is invited to eat in the home of Jethro. The Baal Haturim on Exodus 10:12 states that in the merit of having fed Moses, Jethro's crops were spared from the effects of the plague of locust (I guess he still owned some land in Egypt). He furthermore explains that even an evil person will merit protection because of feeding the righteous. What goes around comes around.

May we always be the vehicle for blessings and protection.

Dedication

To all those who assisted our family during our stay in Montevideo. May you be blessed many times over.

Holy Uruguayan Dogs

"A dog barks when his master is attacked. I would be a coward if I saw that God's truth is attacked and yet would remain silent." -John Calvin

There are a lot of dogs in Uruguay. I don't know how one would determine the statistics, but I would venture to guess that Uruguay has one of the highest number of dogs per capita in the world. The high rate of dog ownership may also contribute to the general easygoing nature of Uruguayans.

The Talmud has a variety of things to say about dogs, but one that the Netziv on Exodus 11:7 highlights are that dogs are spiritually sensitive. In the warning of the upcoming Plague of the Firstborns, Moses states quizzically:

"And for all the Children of Israel, no dog shall whet its tongue, from man to beast, in order that you should know that God differentiates between Egypt and Israel."

The Netziv explains that dogs have the natural ability to differentiate between good people and wicked people. They will bark when confronted with evil. There were immoral people from Israel that God spared during the plagues whom the dogs should have barked at. However, out of respect for God's desire for the national differentiation between Jews and Egyptians, the dogs remained quiet during the historic event of the Exodus and didn't point out the wayward Jews.

Dogs may be man's best friend, but they have also proven to be respectful servants of God. There's a thing or two that we can learn from them.

Dedication

To Uruguayan dogs and your humans. Please remind your caretakers to clean up your messes.

BERESHIT **SHEMOT** VAYIKRA BAMIDBAR DEVARIM   Ibn Ezra
Shemot Va'era **Bo** Beshalach Yitro Mishpatim Terumah Tetzaveh Ki Tisa Vayakhel Pekudei

Bargaining with God

"As I grow older, I pay less attention to what people say. I just watch what they do." -Andrew Carnegie

The roots of commerce must be deeply ingrained in the human psyche. It has become second-nature to want reward or to give reward for products or services. However, when it comes to God, humans have a curiously different approach.

We will call to Him in a time of need. We will pray fervently for His help. We are so desperate for divine assistance that we start to promise things. "God, if you will do x for me, I promise I will do/be y."

Some people take their promises to heart and those are often life-changing events. Many however soon forget their promises once the heavenly boon has been granted.

The Ibn Ezra hints at a more successful approach. He explains (on Exodus 13:8) that though we eat Matza on Passover to commemorate the Exodus from Egypt, in fact, the Matza was the final cause of our liberation. Eating Matza was amongst the first commands God gave the nascent Jewish people. Because they ate the Matza, because they obeyed the word of God, they merited the historic emancipation that created our nation.

God prefers to see those positive acts up front (cash) – He doesn't always grant wishes based on promises for the future (credit).

Dedication

To Rachel and Ariel Tepperman on the birth of their daughter. Mazal Tov!

BERESHIT **SHEMOT** VAYIKRA BAMIDBAR DEVARIM   *Ohr Hachayim*
Shemot Va'era **Bo** *Beshalach Yitro Mishpatim Terumah Tetzaveh Ki Tisa Vayakhel Pekudei*

Everything is Timing

"Time is the coin of your life. It is the only coin you have, and only you can determine how it will be spent. Be careful lest you let other people spend it for you."

Carl Sandburg (1878 – 1967)

The Jewish laws have a love affair with punctiliousness. One minute a person can be fulfilling a commandment, but if you're a minute too early or too late, you may warrant a death penalty (yes, harsh religion too).

In the story of the Exodus, the Ohr Hachayim (Exodus 12:17) brings our attention to one of many unusual verses:

"And you shall guard the Matzot *(unleavened bread)."*

The Ohr Hachayim describes two time elements within the Matzo that we must guard for. One is that it needs to be baked within a very precise period of time (not more than 18 minutes) and it has to be eaten precisely on Passover. The Ohr Hachayim explains that the lessons contained within this verse refer to timing. Just as God was precise in the timing of the redemption of the Children of Israel from their Egyptian bondage, so too we must be precise in our timely performance of His commands to us.

While the above verse deals with Passover, the same can be said regarding the laws of the Sabbath, Yom Kippur, Prayer, Ritual Purity, Marriage, Festivals, and much, much more in Judaism.

For many aspects of the commandments, timing is not only everything, it is the only thing.

May we make correct and timely use of our time.

Dedication

To Moshe Feiglin and Davidi Pearl. My choice of candidates for the upcoming Likud primaries and the Gush Etzion Regional Council, respectively. Don't forget the vote. Use that time wisely!

בשלח

Beshalach

[Exodus Chapters XIII-XVII]

BERESHIT **SHEMOT** VAYIKRA BAMIDBAR DEVARIM Baal Haturim
Shemot Va'era Bo **Beshalach** *Yitro Mishpatim Terumah Tetzaveh Ki Tisa Vayakhel Pekudei*

Choose Your Weapon Carefully
Prayer is not an old woman's idle amusement. Properly understood and applied, it is the most potent instrument of action. -Mahatma Gandhi

The People of Israel have finally been redeemed from the enslavement of Egypt. They have marched through the desert. They reach the edge of the sea and suddenly find themselves pursued by the entire armed might of the Egyptian empire.

They panic. They cry. They scream. They complain. Moses calls out to God. God, in one of His most famous and indicative statements replies: **"Why do you call out to Me? Speak to the Children of Israel and Go!"**

The Baal Haturim on Exodus 14:15 teases out an important lesson from God's response. There are times for long prayer, like the forty days and nights that Moses spent on Mount Sinai praying for forgiveness for the sin of the Golden Calf. There are times for short prayers, like the five words Moses uttered when praying for the health of his sister, Miriam. And then, there are times when no words are appropriate, but rather action is called for.

May we choose our strategies correctly, the right prayer or action for the right circumstances.

Dedication
To the entire Jewish community of Uruguay. Your hosting of our family has been exemplary. May all our prayers be answered.

Liar's Reward

"Falsehood is invariably the child of fear in one form or another." - Aleister Crowley

The adage of the boy who cried wolf is important and well-known, however, the Netziv has a slightly different take on it.

The nation of Israel has escaped from the centuries of Egyptian slavery. God parted the sea for them, allowing them to miraculously walk on dry land and see the Egyptian military annihilated. The Israelites walk through the desert, find a stream of bitter waters and then Moses is directed to put nearby trees in the water, thereby sweetening the stream and providing water to the entire nation.

However, a chapter later, the Israelites find themselves again without water, but this time the interplay is different. They complain that they have no water. Moses is not impressed by their complaint. Only after they complain does the text say that the people were thirsty. The Netziv on the verse (Exodus 17:3) explains that though they lacked water they complained before they became thirsty. And so, the false complaint of thirst came true. He then expands that whoever fakes a complaint, eventually it will become true.

A person who claims to not have money, will eventually see that fulfilled. A person who lies about his inability to do something, eventually will lose that ability. A boy who cries wolf, not only will he not be believed, but eventually will have his false statement made true and bring a wolf upon himself.

May we be very careful about our claims and statements, lest they become true.

Dedication

To truth-speakers. May only blessings be your reward.

BERESHIT **SHEMOT** VAYIKRA BAMIDBAR DEVARIM   Ibn Ezra
Shemot Va'era Bo **Beshalach** Yitro Mishpatim Terumah Tetzaveh Ki Tisa Vayakhel Pekudei

Why Seven Days?

"Time is the most valuable coin in your life. You and you alone will determine how that coin will be spent. Be careful that you don't let other people spend it for you." -John Dryden

A seven-day week does not reflect any natural phenomena. As opposed to a day, a lunar month or a solar year, a week is an artificial creation.

Some interesting exceptions to the seven-day week include the Igbo people of Nigeria (4 days), the Javanese of Indonesia (5 days) and the Akans of West Africa (6 days that have been mixed with a 7-day week giving a 42-day cycle).

Historically, the Romans had an 8-day week for a time, until they met the 7-day week which became more popular. Both ancient China and Egypt had a 10-day week. In more modern times, during the excitement of revolution, the French adopted a 10-day week. It lasted for nine and a half years (1793-1802). The Soviets experimented with a 5-day week from 1929-31 and then tried a 6-day week until 1940. None of these counting systems have survived.

Why does almost all of humanity follow a 7-day week? Ibn Ezra claims (Exodus 16:1) that it comes from the Torah. God mandated a 7-day week to remember Creation as well as to remember the Exodus. Curious how the entire world has adopted this Jewish tradition – in most cases without even knowing it.

I wonder what other traditions have permeated the world and which others may still do so?

Dedication

To Jared Diamond and his glorious book *Guns, Germs and Steel*, where among other things he highlights potential causes as to the fate of societies and civilization.

BERESHIT **SHEMOT** VAYIKRA BAMIDBAR DEVARIM   Ohr Hachayim
Shemot Va'era Bo **Beshalach** Yitro Mishpatim Terumah Tetzaveh Ki Tisa Vayakhel Pekudei

The Physics of Miracles

"A miracle is nothing more or less than this. Anyone who has come into a knowledge of his true identity, of his oneness with the all-pervading wisdom and power, this makes it possible for laws higher than the ordinary mind knows of to be revealed to him."

-Ralph Waldo Trine

Miracles, however we understand them, happen for a reason. By looking deeper into the cause and effect of miracles, one might discover that they actually follow certain patterns, are affected by certain principles, even follow certain rules. Below is a start of a list:

1. *Don't make God work too hard.* God prefers to keep certain miracles "private" (i.e. when the prophet Elisha revives the dead boy or when the poor woman receives an abundance of oil, the door is closed in both cases – see II Kings Chapter 4).

2. *Be good.* God may perform miracles for those deserving of it (splitting of the Reed Sea – Ohr Hachayim Exodus 14:15).

3. *Learn Torah.* God is said to have created the world using the Torah as a "blueprint." Those who master the Torah may wield some power over creation (Moses mastering the sea – Ohr Hachayim Exodus 14:27).

4. *Knowing the mind of God.* God did **not** command that the Jews refrain from leaving anything over from the daily Manna. It was an innovation Moses introduced, understanding God's intention. God approved of Moses' command and performed a miracle to "back him up" whereby worms ate whatever Manna was left over the next day (Ohr Hachayim Exodus 16:19).

There are more rules and regulations as to how miracles work, but this list is a good start: don't make a show (when not needed), be good, study Torah and know God.

May we all merit seeing miracles every day of our lives.

Dedication

To the miracle of rain. After many relatively dry years, Israel had the wettest January on record (at least 26 days) and it has raised the water-level of the Kinneret (our main reservoir) by 55 centimeters in January. Currently it stands at -213.11 centimeters, which is 11 centimeters below the Kinneret's red line.

יתרו

Yitro

[Exodus Chapters XVIII-XX]

BERESHIT **SHEMOT** VAYIKRA BAMIDBAR DEVARIM　　Baal Haturim
Shemot Va'era Bo Beshalach **Yitro** Mishpatim Terumah Tetzaveh Ki Tisa Vayakhel Pekudei

Delayed Repercussions

Sooner or later everyone sits down to a banquet of consequences. – Robert Louis Stevenson

Moses arrives in a strange land. He has escaped his birthplace of Egypt. He has left his birth-nation of Israel. He finds himself amongst the idolaters of Midian and hosted by their High Priest, Jethro. Jethro appears to be a kindly, wise man. He gives Moses his daughter in marriage. However, the two men come from very different cultures and traditions, and that is where the trouble begins.

Moses comes from a monotheistic religion that believes in the one, unseen, all-powerful God. Jethro serves man-made idols. They both realize the importance of educating children. The midrash states that Moses made a deal with Jethro. Moses promised that his first son would be raised in the ways of idol worship (keep in mind this happens before the initial encounter of Moses and God at the burning bush). However, the Baal Haturim on Exodus 18:3 explains that Moses expected the wise Jethro to finally understand the error of his idolatrous ways and allow the son of Moses to be raised according to the Jewish faith.

That is indeed what happens, but the Baal Haturim says that the damage was already done, though we are not to see the results until the following generation. At the end of the book of Judges there is a not-so-subtle hint that the grandson of Moses becomes a High Priest to idol worship. The deal, even though apparently annulled was fulfilled anyway, not with a son, but with a grandson.

May we be cautious of the deals we get into or hope to get out of. They have a way of biting you when you least expect it.

Dedication

To my brother-in-law, Rabbi Daniel Epstein, on his induction as Rabbi of Cockfosters and N Southgate Synagogue. May it be a deal they and the community enjoy for a long time.

Preparing for God

"Spectacular achievement is always preceded by spectacular preparation." -Robert H. Schuller

Athletes are obvious examples of people who need to prepare excessively to succeed. But serious preparation is a prerequisite for success in almost every aspect of life. For any profession, for any business, for any task, for any relationship, there needs to be time and effort invested to reap the fruits of triumph.

Spiritual life is no different. To have and enjoy a rich spiritual life requires preparation. It requires work, commitment and perseverance. It doesn't just happen.

At the giving of the Ten Commandments, the Jewish people are about to stand in the presence of God in the most powerful and direct revelation in the history of the world. One might think that just the essence of such a concentrated display of God would be enough. Nonetheless, the Jewish nation is instructed to prepare themselves already three days before the singular event. The Netziv on Exodus 19:2 explains that the more one prepares himself for the encounter with the divine, the more it will take hold in their being.

However, on Exodus 19:11 the Netziv gives a warning regarding the same theme. He claims that if one does not prepare enough, one can leave such holy encounters damaged, even deranged. This is not meant to scare people away from spiritual encounters – it is meant to show the importance and value of preparing for them.

Feel free to contact me for more customized preparation directions.

Dedication

To Olympic athletes. There is something inspiring about their dedication to their goals.

BERESHIT **SHEMOT** VAYIKRA BAMIDBAR DEVARIM   Ibn Ezra
Shemot Va'era Bo Beshalach **Yitro** Mishpatim Terumah Tetzaveh Ki Tisa Vayakhel Pekudei

Hold Thy God

"It chills my blood to hear the blest Supreme rudely appealed to on each trifling theme." -William Cowper

The Third Commandment of the famous Ten seems oddly underwhelming. One and Two are the fundamentals of faith (Belief in God and Not Believing in Other gods). Four and Five are Keeping the Sabbath and Honoring ones Parents – fundamentals of Judaism. Six through Ten deal with the underpinnings of a healthy and functional society, Don't Kill, Don't Steal, etc. So why is number Three, Not Uttering God's Name in Vain, so prominent on the list? What's the big deal about a phrase that has become second nature to many people?

Ibn Ezra (on Exodus 20:7) claims that it is its very ease of violating that has placed Do Not Utter God's Name in Vain so highly and that in fact in a certain way it is more important and its effects more dangerous and corrosive than murder, theft or adultery (this does not now become a license in any way to commit any of the above).

The obvious sins, one may often be fearful of doing. One might get caught. But a simple utterance that does not bother or offend most people is easy to do – even unthinkingly. The problem is that flippant use of God's name consistently erodes ones view and relationship with God. God becomes merely another word, another phrase in the arsenal of our vocabulary. God loses meaning. God loses significance. The entire foundation of ones belief and worship may disintegrate as would a termite-infested house. All the other commandments become meaningless when we lose the proper perspective vis-à-vis God.

Ergo, Don't Take His Name in Vain.

Dedication

To the memory of Hanan Einav-Levy, a man who passed away in the prime of his life. I never had the pleasure to meet Hanan, but have been inspired by his work in wind energy and his dedication to the future of Israel.

BERESHIT **SHEMOT** VAYIKRA BAMIDBAR DEVARIM　　*Ohr Hachayim*
Shemot Va'era Bo Beshalach **Yitro** Mishpatim Terumah Tetzaveh Ki Tisa Vayakhel Pekudei

Homemade Deities

"The worshiper is the father of the gods." – H. L. Mencken (1880 – 1956)

Captain Kirk and the landing party of the Starship Enterprise were trapped on a planet, captives of an entity that claimed to be nothing less than the Greek god Apollo. He claimed to be the last of his space-faring race that thousands of years before had landed on Earth and were accepted as gods by the primitive Greeks.

Kirk figured out that the source of Apollo's power was that the humans "believed" in him. When Kirk and crew "unbelieved" in him, Apollo vanished into nothingness (see Star Trek "Who Mourns for Adonais" Episode #33).

It has been the theme of more than one fantasy and sci-fi novel, film or show that a so-called "god" draws his power from people who "believe" in him. The Ohr Hachayim (Exodus 20:3), in a parallel concept claims that a person, just by giving thought and credence to strange gods, in effect brings them to life (hence idol worship is the only punishable thought-sin).

He seems to say that our thought processes in this realm, in the realm of belief and worship create a new reality. By idolizing foreign concepts, passing beliefs and transient figures we give power and bring into existence something that shouldn't be part of our world.

May we stay clear of false gods and their ephemeral power.

Dedication

To Boaz and Nechama Spitz on the birth of their daughter (and my niece) Ariel Aliza (she is rumored to have god-like power). Wishing them much joy, health and happiness.

משפטים

Mishpatim

[Exodus Chapters XXI-XXIV]

BERESHIT **SHEMOT** VAYIKRA BAMIDBAR DEVARIM　　Baal Haturim
Shemot Va'era Bo Beshalach Yitro **Mishpatim** Terumah Tetzaveh Ki Tisa Vayakhel Pekudei

Smooth Talkers

We kill everybody, my dear. Some with bullets, some with words, and everybody with our deeds. We drive people into their graves, and neither see it nor feel it. -Maxim Gorky

There are people, who through the power of their personality, their charisma and their eloquence can get unsuspecting victims to do something of their own free will that may go against their own interests and well-being. The reason they are influential is because humans on a whole are a trusting species. Our society would disintegrate if the foundation of trust did not underlie basic human interactions.

However, there are some opportunists that take advantage of this visceral trust, play upon people's feelings and beliefs and sell them something which is simply not real, not true. The Baal Haturim on Exodus 21:14 compares these smooth talkers to false prophets. The false prophet would often prophecy what the people wanted to hear. They would soothe their fears and not confront them with the reality ahead. Not warn them of the error of their ways in time for them to correct it and save themselves. The false prophets doomed themselves and their followers to oblivion.

The Baal Haturim compares both the smooth talkers and the false prophets to murderers. By betraying the trust people put in them, they are killing them. They are destroying the relationship of trust that connects them to life. In some cases they even lead them to actual death.

May truth and honesty always be our hallmark.

Dedication

To the honest people in our lives. You are a beacon in an often hazy and dark world.

Cursing's Legacy

"I believe that what we become depends on what our fathers teach us at odd moments, when they aren't trying to teach us." -Umberto Eco

It is often something of a national pastime to criticize and even curse our leaders. They are easy punching-bags upon which to vent all of our complaints and grievances with the world. Even if the faults are true, there is little that such grumblings accomplish.

The Torah warns us against cursing ones rulers. The Netziv learns at least two lessons from that particular commandment. On Exodus 22:27 he states that the prohibition against cursing the leadership is specified exactly because it is so easy, natural and common. The second lesson is a bit deeper with longer-term implications.

On Exodus 22:28 the Netziv prophesizes that a man who refrains from cursing his leaders, whether they be political or religious, will merit to have a son who will himself serve God via lay or religious leadership. There is something in the act of showing restraint, respect and deference to our leadership that cultivates and empowers the next generation to take on the mantle of leadership.

If leaders are the subject of constant disparagement at home, why would any child, even unconsciously, seek or even consider higher ambitions? Just so that he should become a subject of idle discussion and inane criticism? No. It is only the child that is spared and shielded from such negativity that dares rise above the mundane, and in the words of the Mishna, "Be a man where there are no men."

May we help cultivate future leaders.

Dedication

To the Jewish lay leadership of Uruguay, and specifically to Sara Winkowski, the force behind the successful introduction of the pre-nuptial solution, who never gave up on her mission. I am constantly humbled and inspired by the leadership's dedication to the community.

Divine Moisturizer

"You can free yourself from aging by reinterpreting your body and by grasping the link between belief and biology."-Deepak Chopra

The clock of our doom starts ticking from the moment of our birth. Our genetic program will determine our height, health and longevity. There seems to be little one may do to extend ones natural lifespan, while there is no lack of factors that will shorten our lives.

Ibn Ezra (on Exodus 23:26) rejects such deterministic views. He claims and provides a physical explanation as to how a person can extend the life they were born to have.

He states that a body will live as long as it has internal heat and moisture. Once the heat and moisture run out, the body dies. Artificial additions of these physical measures will not help. But there is one thing that can: cleaving to God. The metaphysical dynamics are as follows: Attaching oneself to God increases the "heat" and "moisture" of the spirit. The "heat" and "moisture" of the spirit are then converted into real heat and moisture in our bodies that will prolong physical biological life beyond its original program. A cold, dry spirit withers. A warm, fluid soul flourishes.

Ibn Ezra states further that not only will clinging to God extend ones natural life, but it can also safeguard a person from accidents and epidemics that may curtail life.

I'm willing to work on it…

Dedication

To the memory of Seymour Hirschfield, father of our friend and neighbor Zvi (Hal) Hirschfield.

You get what you pay for...

"Labor is still, and ever will be, the inevitable price set upon everything which is valuable." -Samuel Smiles

Supply and demand is a fact of economic life. If labor is cheap in Malaysia, if there are product overruns from Nestle, then why shouldn't the consumer benefit by cheap prices? However, I've always suspected there is something inherently evil in extreme imbalances in economic systems. Somehow the cheapness of a product, the cheapness of labor, diminishes the value of work or the value of a person. It is reflected in a culture of cutting corners, of tainted milk from China, of maltreatment of workers throughout the globe.

The Ohr Hachayim (Exodus 21:4) develops an interesting corollary in our fulfillment of commandments. To perform commandments, takes time, effort and typically money. Kosher food is often more expensive, a Jewish education is certainly exorbitant (outside of Israel), not working on the Sabbath is a loss of income. Living by the commandments is an investment. It's not always easy and it is rarely cheap (especially when time is money). However, there is an interesting solace to our financial and time investment.

The Ohr Hachayim explains that there is a certain evil spirit that floats around us. It can only attach itself to things that are free or cheap. But commandments that we need to work on, that we spend money on, the evil spirit can't touch. Evil cannot attach itself to anything of true value, anything that we sweated over, that we invested in.

May we have the ability to fulfill commandments and may they always be blessed.

Dedication

To the launch of the Times of Israel — A serious investment — may no evil touch it.

תרומה

Terumah

[Exodus Chapters XXV-XXVII]

BERESHIT **SHEMOT** VAYIKRA BAMIDBAR DEVARIM   Baal Haturim
Shemot Va'era Bo Beshalach Yitro Mishpatim **Terumah** Tetzaveh Ki Tisa Vayakhel Pekudei

Bread of Faith

There is hunger for ordinary bread, and there is hunger for love, for kindness, for thoughtfulness; and this is the great poverty that makes people suffer so much. -Mother Theresa

The Baal Haturim on Exodus 26:9 states that in the merit of the service of the Table of the Showbread in the Temple, the entire world was bestowed with blessings.

Story: A simple baker was reading the Torah portion. He read about the Showbread that the priests placed in the Temple every week. He felt bad for God that since the destruction of the Temple, nobody was giving God bread anymore. He decided that in honor of the Sabbath, he would place two loaves of Challah, the traditional bread for the Sabbath, in the Ark of the Torah in the synagogue. He was so excited about his decision, he woke up before dawn Friday morning and placed the very first loaves he had baked in the Ark, with a short prayer to God to accept his offering.

In the same synagogue there was a poor caretaker who had fallen on hard times. He couldn't afford Challah for that Sabbath. That Thursday night in the synagogue, he cried and pleaded to God to help him; that he should not come to his family empty-handed. As was his ritual, every Friday morning, he cleaned up the synagogue for the Sabbath. He opened the Ark to check on the Torah, and lo and behold! Two warm fresh Challahs were waiting there for him. The caretaker cried for joy, thanking God for this miracle, for remembering him after all and listening to his prayer.

The baker arrived early Friday afternoon to the synagogue, curious as to what had happened to his loaves. He opened the Ark, and to his surprise, the loaves were gone! God had accepted his humble offering! Encouraged, the baker did the same thing the following Friday. The caretaker was humbled and moved each time he found the warm, fresh bread. This cycle continued for months, both the baker and the caretaker filled with an extraordinary joy, yet unaware of each others actions.

One Friday, the Rabbi of the synagogue woke up early and decided to do some studying in the back of the synagogue. Unnoticed, the Rabbi saw the baker bring in his loaves and put them in the Ark and reverently bestow them to God. Later, he saw the caretaker gingerly, lovingly, removing them and thanking God. The Rabbi understood immediately the error these simpletons were making. He called them both and berated them: "You fools! God is not placing or receiving the Challah. It is your own human hands that are responsible." Both the baker and the caretaker stood there ashamed, while their foolishness was brought to light and their simple faith shattered.

BERESHIT **SHEMOT** *VAYIKRA BAMIDBAR DEVARIM*   Baal Haturim
Shemot Va'era Bo Beshalach Yitro Mishpatim **Terumah** *Tetzaveh Ki Tisa Vayakhel Pekudei*

That night, the Prophet Elijah came to the Rabbi in a dream: "You evil man!" Elijah screamed at the Rabbi. "God has not had as much joy in the world, since the service of the Showbread in the Temple was stopped, as when the baker delivered the Challah, and the caretaker received it, and they both displayed a pure, simple faith. Know that the evil you have done cannot be undone and you have caused great anguish to God!"

Sometimes, simple faith is the best.

Dedication

To our baker, Netanel, on his first batch of successful and tasty biscochos!

Portable Honor

"There are three crowns: the crown of Torah, the crown of priesthood, and the crown of royalty. But the crown of a good name is greater than them all." Rabbi Simon, Avot 4:17

God instructs Moses to build the Tabernacle, the portable desert Temple. The people of Israel contribute generously of their time and resources towards its construction. The last part of the Book of Exodus is filled with the details of the building, materials, labor, components, utensils, measurements and final assembly of what is otherwise also known as The Sanctuary.

There were a few components within the Tabernacle that were of particular significance. The most prominent was the Ark of the Covenant that carried the tablets of stone that bore the famed Ten Commandments. The Ark was situated in the innermost chamber of the Sanctuary. Two other components are worth mentioning for their symbolism: the Table and the Altar.

According to the Netziv on Exodus 25:14, the Ark is symbolic of Torah, the Altar is symbolic of the priesthood and the Table is symbolic of kingship. As per Rabbi Simon quoted above, it relates well to the concept of the three crowns and indeed, each of these components (the Ark, Altar and Table) had a raised border that surrounded its upper surface not unlike a large physical crown. The Mishna in Tractate Avot goes on to enumerate how one can attain these metaphorical crowns. Those of priesthood or kingship are by definition only available to a small subset of the people of Israel, but the crown of Torah is available to all.

The Netziv makes another interesting observation. The crowns of kingship and priesthood are not only attainable based on ones lineage, but can also only be reached when the people of Israel are fully established in the land of Israel. However, the crown of Torah can be reached anywhere in the world, independent of the national situation.

May we not only individually find our crowns of Torah, but as a nation may we see the crowns of priesthood and kingship restored speedily in our days.

Dedication

To the Uruguayan parliament, for their meaningful and moving remembrance of the victims of the Holocaust.

BERESHIT **SHEMOT** VAYIKRA BAMIDBAR DEVARIM   Ibn Ezra
Shemot Va'era Bo Beshalach Yitro Mishpatim **Terumah** Tetzaveh Ki Tisa Vayakhel Pekudei

Concentrated Divine Presence

"The only thing that makes one place more attractive to me then another is the quantity of heart I find in it." -Jane Welsh Carlyle

Man is often likened to a universe onto himself. Ibn Ezra relates to this theme often and states that by understanding ones inner workings, a person can often gain insight into the world.

It is agreed that the heart is the primary component for the functioning of the body. It is perhaps the most vital organ, providing life-sustaining force to the rest of the body. The major veins and arteries adjacent to it are likewise critical pathways to the other major organs. The further we get away from the heart, the less the amount of blood that is pumped to far away limbs. There is a greater concentration of life and vitality the closer one gets to the heart.

Ibn Ezra on Exodus 25:40 says that geographically it is the same. The Temple Mount has the most concentrated presence of God on our planet. That is where His heart is. The city of Jerusalem likewise has a high concentration of God's presence and to a lesser extent so does the land of Israel. Outside of Israel, Ibn Ezra argues, God is still present, for He fills the world, but not in the same concentrated fashion.

As they say in the real estate business, the three most important factors are location, location, location.

Dedication

To the memories of Rabbi David Hartman and Israel Ivtzan. They both contributed to the people of Israel with all their heart in their own significant and distinct ways. May their families find comfort amongst the mourners of Zion and Jerusalem.

In honor of the marriage of Shoshi Taragin and Gidon Kupietzky. May they contribute much to the people of Israel in their own way.

BERESHIT **SHEMOT** VAYIKRA BAMIDBAR DEVARIM   Ohr Hachayim
Shemot Va'era Bo Beshalach Yitro Mishpatim **Terumah** Tetzaveh Ki Tisa Vayakhel Pekudei

Plain-Sight Secrets

"Anything will give up its secrets if you love it enough. Not only have I found that when I talk to the little flower or to the little peanut they will give up their secrets, but I have found that when I silently commune with people they give up their secrets also - if you love them enough."

George Washington Carver (1864 - 1943)

Modern literature and film is filled with portrayals of secret societies hiding clues in plain sight. Ancient documents, buildings, or works-of-art hide a secret code that is understandable only to the faithful of the group or those who find the "key" to understand the otherwise inscrutable public message.

The Ohr Hachayim claims there is a real secret code hidden in the plain text of the Bible. In the weekly Torah reading of Terumah, Moses is given the initial instructions for the construction of the Sanctuary and its components in the Sinai Desert. The instructions are often difficult to decipher and at times seems oddly repetitious.

The Sanctuary was constructed as a light, mobile structure, quickly and easily dismantled and reassembled. It was appropriate for the Jewish desert sojourn which often had them relocating on short notice.

The Ohr Hachayim (Exodus Ch. 26) claims however, that the instructions are not only for the Sanctuary, but that also woven within the text are another set of instructions. There is a second, hidden set of instructions, for the construction of the permanent Temple that King Solomon would eventually build in Jerusalem.

It is impossible to understand the second set of instructions just by reading the text. There was a separate "key" that was handed down from Israelite father to son, from teacher to student that enabled them to decipher the otherwise obtuse text. The Ohr Hachayim claims that King David transmitted the key to his son Solomon who then constructed the Temple based on the divine plans.

May those who have the "key" pass it on and may we merit seeing the Temple rebuilt speedily in our days.

Dedication

To the memory of Prof. Cyril Yechiel Domb, FRS. He unlocked multiple secrets within Torah as well as Science.

תצוה

Tetzaveh

[Exodus Chapters XXVII-XXX]

BERESHIT **SHEMOT** VAYIKRA BAMIDBAR DEVARIM   Baal Haturim
Shemot Va'era Bo Beshalach Yitro Mishpatim Terumah **Tetzaveh** Ki Tisa Vayakhel Pekudei

Useless Superstition

Superstition is only the fear of belief, while religion is the confidence. - Marguerite Blessington

There is a common belief in Judaism that the religious article known as a Mezuza, a scroll of parchment with two paragraphs of the Torah written on it, placed on ones doorpost, affords some type of divine protection. A superstitious corollary to that belief is that if something wrong or unfortunate occurs in the home or the family, there may be something faulty with the Mezuza. Indeed, there are startling stories of people who have checked their Mezuza and found an eerie relationship between the fault in the text of their Mezuza and the event that prompted its checking. Going down this road leads to the conclusion that correcting the text of the Mezuza will correct one's life.

I am often approached by people with various mishaps in their lives who ask me to check their Mezuzas. It somehow eludes them that perhaps their leading a life separated from God, separated from morality, separated from the laws and traditions of the Jewish people, may be the more direct cause of divine retribution than any parchment's error.

The Baal Haturim on Exodus 28:32 states that the High Priest had a special garment that somehow did afford protection for punishment for the severe sin of gossiping. But he elaborates that the protection only worked after the offender would stop his gossiping ways and repent. Then and only then would the metaphysical properties of the garment provide protection from punishment.

The causes of our mishaps are usually internal. We don't need to look to Mezuzas, red strings or other mystical solutions to fix the problems inside.

Dedication

To the venerated Chofetz Chaim who made some news this week with the discovery of an old film from 1923 showing him for a few seconds (at 0:57 to be precise).

Spiritual Ingredients

"By the work one knows the workmen." -Jean De La Fontaine

A long time ago in a land far away I had a very special martial arts teacher. Besides his ability to pulverize cinderblocks with a single strike he had an unusual sensitivity to inanimate objects. He could touch, for example, a hand-made knife, and would discern something of the spirit of its creator. Once, he told us, he touched an object which had such a foul spiritual signature that it made him ill.

I have heard of Chassidic Rabbis that also had a similar sensitivity, that by touching a book he could tell something about a person with a strong spiritual aura who had last touched that book. My own extra-sensory perceptions are limited to food. There is something about a home-cooked meal that tastes better than anything commercially or industrially prepared. One can almost taste the love that goes into such cooking.

The Netziv on Exodus 28:3 says that the same spiritual energy and effect occurred with the construction of the Tabernacle as well as with all of the priestly vessels and garments. The artisans who fabricated each component did so with great intent. They placed a part of their soul into their work. Aaron, the High Priest, was able to sense their spirit and purity of purpose which in turn fortified him in his work as the spiritual representative of the Nation of Israel.

May we do the tasks given to us well, do it with spirit. One never knows the reverberations that will be felt, where, when or by whom.

Dedication

To Orlando, our guide of the gold mine in Minas. His love of his task was amazing — and so was the tour of the old mine that was excavated extensively in the 1730s.

Rabbinic Stone Healing

"The art of medicine consists of amusing the patient while nature cures the disease." -Voltaire

Western medicine is typically disparaging of any treatments that cannot be confirmed by a peer-reviewed double-blind study with a well defined control group, often heavily financed by pharmaceutical companies. Eastern medicine on the other hand, forays frequently into the realm of superstition, idol-worship and outright chicanery.

Jewish sages throughout the ages tended to adopt the medical practices of their time and place, and sought where possible to exclude useless or problematic "medical" trends.

Ibn Ezra makes mention of the "powers" of stones which to Western ears may sound like nonsense. However, in his comments on Exodus 28:9, he expands about *"a stone that if worn on a finger, the person will see his dreams. And this should not be a surprise, as each stone has its unique powers. There is a stone that attracts metal, and one that stills the blood, and one that flees from vinegar and one that always breaks into triangles."*

Perhaps there is some truth after all to healing properties of some stones?

Dedication

To the speedy and complete healing of those suffering from all and any illness, especially the flu that seems to be affecting many this season.

Ripped Jeans Philosophy
"The apparel oft proclaims the man."- William Shakespeare

Fashion aficionados can perhaps recall better, but there was a time that ripped jeans became so popular, that people paid for pre-ripped jeans. What may have started as a non-conformist trend (how's that for an oxymoron) developed into the latest fashion statement. People glorified the beat-up look of their attire.

I remember being drawn into the clothing madness. I was relieved when my jeans suffered rips of their own. I proudly left the rips and joined the masses, finally fitting in with all the cool people. I discovered two things very quickly. The first was that the ripped jeans did nothing for my social status. The second was that it was cold and uncomfortable walking around with ripped jeans.

The Ohr Hachayim (1696-1743) gives his own opinion as to ripped garments. In describing the priestly garments, the Bible declares that they should be "for honor and splendor." The Ohr Hachayim (Exodus 28:40) connects this statement to the Talmud (Tractate Zvachim 18b) which explains that if a priest served in the Temple with ripped or disheveled clothing he was disqualified and his service was voided.

When serving God, we need to do so in clean, dignified and whole clothing, no matter what the latest fashion may be.

May we always be well attired.

Dedication
To Sharon Katz and the whole crew of Dames of the Dance for their incredible efforts: "Strength and dignity are her clothing; and she laughs at the time to come."

כי תשא

Ki Tisa

[Exodus Chapters XXX-XXXIV]

BERESHIT **SHEMOT** VAYIKRA BAMIDBAR DEVARIM   Baal Haturim
Shemot Va'era Bo Beshalach Yitro Mishpatim Terumah Tetzaveh **Ki Tisa** Vayakhel Pekudei

The Labor of Thinking

It is the power of thought that gives man power over nature. -Hans Christian Andersen

There is a common misconception of Jewish Law that on the Sabbath one needs to refrain from manual labor. The legal biblical term is "melacha" which would be more appropriately translated as any "creative action." Hence, such mundane and non-taxing actions such as tying a knot, dividing materials, writing and much more are prohibited on the Sabbath, though there is little or no exertion.

The Baal Haturim highlights another aspect of "melacha" that should be refrained from. He claims on Exodus 31:4 that even "thinking" is a form of "melacha." Now he does not mean the natural brain processes that occur whenever we are conscious and perform any action or have any thought. He is referring to the thinking that is behind any constructive, creative, work-related thought that we are usually busy with throughout the work week.

On the Sabbath, he is telling us to refrain from even "thinking" about our work. There is something against the laws and especially the spirit of the Sabbath, to be preoccupied, to consider, to review, to plan or to have anything to do, even in the solitude of our own minds with "melacha." Our brains, our emotions and our spirits will thank you for the weekly, enriching, invigorating, rejuvenating and healing respite.

p.s. For anyone interested in more details on what is and isn't "melacha" don't hesitate to contact me.

Dedication

To the new President of Uruguay, Tabaré Vázquez. May he give much thought to his leadership of the country.

Complete Dedication

"Your powers are dead or dedicated. If they are dedicated, they are alive with God and tingle with surprising power. If they are saved up, taken care of for their own ends, they are dead." -Eli Stanley Jones

In this Olympic season, it is inspiring to see the commitment, the dedication of athletes for their chosen goals. It is entertaining to see the seriousness with which they pursue their sports and the honor the winners receive.

However, when the Children of Israel rebel against God, by worshipping the Golden Calf, there is a much more serious game afoot. Moses basically calls for a civil war, adjuring his followers that "brother shall kill brother." At the end, only the members of Moses' own tribe, the Levites, join him. It would seem a battle fraught with danger. The members of one small tribe against wild, idolatrous masses from the rest of Israel.

The Torah recounts the casualty list at the end of the battle. Three thousand of the idol worshippers were slain. None of the Levites are reported as fallen. The Netziv on Exodus 32:26 wonders as to the extreme imbalance in the casualties of war. How did a much smaller force not lose a man while the larger rabble suffered what amounted to a massacre? (see the dramatization in my fictional account)

The Netziv explains that the answer can be found in the nature of Moses' call for troops: "Whoever is for God, to me!" To the Netziv, it is more than a powerful rallying call. It is a selection criteria. Moses is recruiting those who are "for God" – but **only** "for God." In this battle there was no room for those of mixed allegiance. There was no place for those who had doubts about God or were not wholly dedicated to Him. Only the purely devoted could fight, should fight and furthermore, because of their loyalty need not fear any hurt in the violent confrontation.

May we find and increase our dedication and thereby vanquish our fears.

Dedication

To the memory of Jacky Amzallag. I never met a man more dedicated to a synagogue than he was. His example was an inspiration. May his family be comforted amongst the mourners of Zion and Jerusalem.

BERESHIT **SHEMOT** VAYIKRA BAMIDBAR DEVARIM   *Ibn Ezra*
Shemot Va'era Bo Beshalach Yitro Mishpatim Terumah Tetzaveh **Ki Tisa** Vayakhel Pekudei

Win Friends and Influence People

"Remember that a man's name is to him the sweetest and most important sound in any language." -Dale Carnegie, How to Win Friends and Influence People

Dale Carnegie, in his bestselling book quoted above, posits the importance of calling a person by their name. Ibn Ezra (on Exodus 31:2), many hundreds of years earlier, makes the same point and takes it a step further.

When choosing the Master Architect for the Tabernacle, God says: *"See, I have called by name, Bezalel..."* Ibn Ezra explains that God's "calling by name" is a supreme honor, one that elevates and gives distinction to the one being named. Bezalel, due to his talents, was uniquely qualified for the role of Master Architect and was therefore worthy of "being called by name."

May we be worthy, and may we likewise find all those around us worthy of being called by name.

Dedication

To my cousins, Ronnen and Iris Rosenthal, on the birth of the first grandchild! The girl has been named Naomi by her parents, Batya and Aharon Castle. Mazal Tov to the entire family!

BERESHIT **SHEMOT** VAYIKRA BAMIDBAR DEVARIM   *Ohr Hachayim*
Shemot Va'era Bo Beshalach Yitro Mishpatim Terumah Tetzaveh **Ki Tisa** Vayakhel Pekudei

Otherworld Practice

"Ninety-nine percent of who you are is invisible and untouchable."
-Richard Buckminster Fuller

The laws of the Sabbath have always seemed strange to me. There is a general prohibition against "work." However, Jewish law has a curious definition of what "work" entails. It includes creative activity but excludes heavy lifting in your own domain. One can legally lift and carry the couch from the living room down to the basement the entire day. You can work hard, sweat, pull your back, and while it is certainly not in the spirit of the Sabbath – no "work" prohibition has been violated. However, the simple, painless and effortless act of flicking a light switch is considered "work" and a violation of the Sabbath.

The Ohr Hachayim (Exodus 31:16) has a novel explanation of what the underlying prohibition of "work" on the Sabbath is. He claims that the main prohibition is one of "thought." Any creative thought, even the turning on of a light, affects the Sabbath spirit. The prohibitions of the Sabbath are meant to give our spirits a rest. There is a fundamental reason our spirits need such a rest. He claims it is a preparation for the afterlife.

There is a belief that on the Sabbath an extra spirit rests on a person. This spirit is ones connection to the upper world, the next world, the afterlife. On the Sabbath we get to practice for the real thing. The next world is meant to be one of enjoyment (within fairly defined and circumscribed conditions) and repose – the time for action and creativity will be over.

Those who train and restrain themselves from creative "work" should have an easy time "adjusting" to the afterlife. Those who haven't rested on the Sabbath as prescribed will find it much more challenging at that next stage.

May we enjoy our bit of the afterlife in this world.

Dedication

To my nephew, Avrumi Spitz, on his Bar-Mitzvah this Shabbat. We look forward to an exciting and otherworldly event.

ויקהל

Vayakhel

[Exodus Chapters XXXV-XXXVIII]

BERESHIT **SHEMOT** VAYIKRA BAMIDBAR DEVARIM   Baal Haturim
Shemot Va'era Bo Beshalach Yitro Mishpatim Terumah Tetzaveh Ki Tisa **Vayakhel** Pekudei

Wise Wives

Marriage is the best state for man in general, and every man is a worse man in proportion to the level he is unfit for marriage. -Samuel Johnson

Voluntary single-hood is at a historic high. People in countries all over the world, of their own free will are making the decision that they do not wish to marry, they do not wish to be joined in matrimony, to share their lives with a significant other. I am not talking about people who have been searching for a spouse for years. I am not talking about people who due to various constraints would have difficulty finding or keeping a mate. I am talking about healthy, well-adjusted, capable people, who seem to think that the best course of action for them and for the world is to remain single for the rest of their lives.

This is probably one of the worst decisions they will make for themselves and for humanity in general. The very first command of God to humanity is to marry and bear children. The Talmud states that a man that is not married is considered dead in some respects. The Baal Haturim on Exodus 35:25 goes a step further and states that one who is married to a wise woman, that woman is credited for giving life to her husband.

May we find, keep and cherish the wise wives we need and may our womenfolk always be the sagacious spouses we rely on.

Dedication
To Tamara

Spoils of the Sabbath

"What is without periods of rest will not endure." –Ovid

A day of rest has become a fairly common phenomenon. This was not always so. For most people, the weekly day off is seen as a time to relax, to have fun, to bond with family and friends and to enjoy life after a hard work-week.

However, there are two types of people who don't enjoy the Sabbath. The first are those that feel the economic distress that prompts them to continue working. The second are workaholics. However, Jewish tradition advises them to take a break as well. Rest is not optional – it's a requirement.

The Netziv on Exodus 35:2 takes the business of rest seriously and explains that not only are those who work on the Sabbath committing a sin, but that they will see no gain, no satisfaction, no benefit from their work. He brings an unusual example from the Israelite conquest of the Canaanite city of Jericho more than 3,000 years ago. According to tradition, the city was conquered on the Sabbath and the Jewish leader, Joshua, disciple of Moses, commanded the Jewish army not to touch any of the spoils of war.

One man however, didn't listen to Joshua and did abscond some of the Jericho treasure. The next Israelite battle was a disaster as a direct result of the infraction of the lone Israelite. The Sabbath-taken treasure was cursed and affected the entire nation. The man who had taken the treasure was subsequently killed together with his entire family.

According to the Netziv (and many others), Sabbath-gained gains will do no good, and may even be cursed.

Workers beware.

Dedication

To Kickstarter. They have a fantastic funding platform for making work projects fun, collaborative and successful.

Temple Fast-Pass

"People don't go there anymore. It's too crowded." -Yogi Berra

Disney World's Magic Kingdom in Florida is the world's most visited attraction with 17 million annual visitors to that park alone. Disney has four theme parks, two water parks, twenty-four themed resorts, five golf courses and more, manned by 66,000 employees, all in the Orlando area.

Because of the incredible masses of people going through their doors, Disney World has become expert at crowd control. There is entertainment while one waits on line. There are "Fast-Pass" options for the discerning visitor. There are strategies for navigating the rides and lines in optimal time. There are books on strategies for beating the lines. There are websites that outdo the popular books with even newer strategies and analysis to maximize the precious time one has in the dream land of Disney.

However, looking more closely at the numbers gives the Magic Kingdom a daily average attendance of merely 40,000. The Tabernacle in the desert had 600,000 men descending upon it on the same day. There wasn't enough space there for all of them!

Ibn Ezra on Exodus 35:20 explains very simply that they came in smaller groups and each group took its turn. It seems we had crowd control even back then.

May we join crowds and wait on lines only for truly positive things (or extremely fun rides).

Dedication
To my in-laws, lovers of all things Disney.

BERESHIT **SHEMOT** VAYIKRA BAMIDBAR DEVARIM　　Ohr Hachayim
Shemot Va'era Bo Beshalach Yitro Mishpatim Terumah Tetzaveh Ki Tisa **Vayakhel** Pekudei

Vital Sermons

"The difference between listening to a radio sermon and going to church...is almost like the difference between calling your girl on the phone and spending an evening with her." - Dwight L. Moody

I admit that I'm a narcoleptic when it comes to Rabbi's sermons. There is something about a Rabbi's voice that is often soothing to the point of unconsciousness. Once in a while, if I'm particularly well rested, or if the speaker is particularly entertaining, I manage to pay attention and join in on that aspect of the communal experience.

However, nowhere in the prayer book does it say: "Rabbi speaks here." The liturgy does not request or even suggest the Rabbi pontificate in front of a captive audience. Some congregations have even done away with the Rabbi's sermon.

The Ohr Hachayim, however, felt very strongly about the Rabbi's sermon and claims that it is actually at the level of a command. He learns it from the gathering Moses convenes (Exodus 35:1) and explains that just as Moses gathered the children of Israel to give them a sermon, so too we are obligated to congregate every Sabbath and listen to the Rabbi's sermon. He even claims that such an endeavor has a redemptive effect upon the congregation.

May we have opportunity to hear our Rabbi's sermons and have the strength to listen to them.

Dedication

To the now forgotten William Eugene Blackstone, author of the proto-Zionist Blackstone Memorial of 1891, one of the earliest Christian Zionists, who was heavily influenced by Dwight L. Moody, quoted above. Blackstone had a strong positive impact on the international Zionist effort, leading to the eventual establishment of the State of Israel.

פקודי

Pekudei

[Exodus Chapters XXXVIII-XL]

BERESHIT **SHEMOT** VAYIKRA BAMIDBAR DEVARIM   **Netziv**
Shemot Va'era Bo Beshalach Yitro Mishpatim Terumah Tetzaveh Ki Tisa Vayakhel **Pekudei**

Blessed Intuition

"Intuition comes very close to clairvoyance; it appears to be the extrasensory perception of reality." -Alexis Carrel

There is a space in any creative work where one finds oneself "in the zone". The "zone" is an almost mythological place for creators, a location in time and space where ones mind, hands and heart are unified and focused in a blissful moment of purpose and concentration of such ease and effortlessness that one becomes unified with the universe at that moment. There is a rightness about such an instant that is heavenly, and affirms our place in the cosmos, if only for a few fleeting minutes.

Bezalel, the head architect of the desert Tabernacle, is credited with having received divine wisdom which allowed him the insights necessary to construct the unique and complex Tabernacle with its multiplicity of parts, components and utensils. At the end of the Book of Exodus, during the description of the completed structure, there is an unusual repetition of the fact that the Tabernacle was constructed according to divine instructions.

The Netziv comments on Exodus 39:43 that the reason for the repetition was because of a sense of surprise. Moses is surprised that Bezalel got all the details right, without having received the minute instructions and subsequent corrections that Moses thought he would have to convey. The Netziv further explains that Bezalel was able to figure out the correct details by looking within himself and having pure intentions. That combination gave him the insight and the intuition to know exactly what to do.

May we learn to tap into our own blessed intuitions.

Dedication

To Ryan and Jordan Brenner and their new art business: La Sombra Gallery

In memory of famed Uruguayan artist, Carlos Páez Vilaró.

ויקרא

Vayikra

[Leviticus Chapters I-V]

The Guilt Offering

Guilt upon the conscience, like rust upon iron, both defiles and consumes it, gnawing and creeping into it, as that does which at last eats out the very heart and substance of the metal. -Bishop Robert South

In Temple times, there were a number of different sacrifices that one could bring. There was the sin-offering, meant as a direct expiation for particular sins. There was the thanksgiving-offering, which as the name implies was offered when we were particularly grateful for something in our lives. There were also the celebratory sacrifices meant to be shared with friends and family on joyous occasions.

One unusual sacrifice was the guilt-offering, which in essence was a very public, physical admission of guilt for a particular failing from a list of sins. We no longer have the sacrifices, but we still have the possibility, requirement and necessity to admit our guilt. In Hebrew, the term is "Vidui". In English, the closest translation is "confession." In Jewish law, the first requirement is to admit guilt to ourselves. Thereafter, Vidui is a regular fixture in our prayers to God. The Rabbis conveniently gave us an alphabetical menu of possible sins that are said daily. On Yom Kippur we have a much more extensive and detailed list of transgressions we confess to and request forgiveness for. Admission of guilt does not necessarily bestow forgiveness, but it is a necessary first step to any possible amends and healing.

While we don't have the Christian tradition of the confessional, there is probably something healthy in admitting our failings to another trusted and understanding soul. The Baal Haturim on Leviticus 4:12 states that no one should be embarrassed to confess their sins, as even the High Priest himself is instructed to publicly bring his own guilt-offering. If that most holy man is capable of sinning and has the obligation to confess and repent, despite the shame, so too the rest of us mortals must have the courage to face our darker side and bring it to the light, in intelligent, healing and productive ways.

May we thereby dispel the demons of guilt that may haunt us and remove that weight from our shoulders, that cancer from our souls.

Dedication
To my friend, the Archbishop of Montevideo, Daniel Sturla, on his recent appointment as Cardinal.

Selfless Self-prayer

"Let everyone try and find that as a result of daily prayer he adds something new to his life, something with which nothing can be compared." -Mahatma Gandhi

Jewish liturgy is often written in the plural form. We should have others in mind in our prayers. Therefore, one might develop feelings of guilt if one were to pray for oneself. How selfish would that be?

The Book of Leviticus presents us with a variety of sacrifices that are brought in the Tabernacle and were subsequently offered in the Temple of Jerusalem.

The Netziv on Leviticus 1:2 explains, as do most Rabbinic commentators, that prayer is a substitute for the sacrifices that were offered. However, he adds, that just as the penitent brings his own sacrifice, so it is with prayer. It is always most effective and appropriate when the person seeking divine assistance prays for himself.

However, there are sacrifices that the spiritual leadership brings on behalf of the people. According to the Netziv, this parallels the ability of a person who doesn't know how to pray to ask the community leadership to pray on his behalf.

We should develop our prayer abilities, and for those of us feeling deficient in that area – find someone who can help us in that department.

Dedication

To the beginning of the Uruguayan school and work year. Feel free to join us at the synagogue for community prayer.

To Betty and Wolf Gruenberg on their wonderful hosting. May all their prayers be answered.

BERESHIT SHEMOT **VAYIKRA** BAMIDBAR DEVARIM   Ibn Ezra
Vayikra Tzav Shemini Tazria Metzora Acharei Mot Kedoshim Emor Behar Bechukotai

Carnivorous God
"The key to faith is what we are willing to sacrifice to obtain it." -Elder Cloward

A significant portion of the Torah concerns itself with sacrifices, specifically animal sacrifices. There are chapters and chapters that go on about what type of animal should be offered on the altar, for what circumstances and with what accompanying service.

In our day and age the concept of animal sacrifice seems primitive and barbaric, yet it occupied a central part of Jewish practice for thousands of years. What was so vital about offering unblemished, productive animals in the prime of their lives to an apparently ravenous God?

Ibn Ezra (Leviticus 1:1) accentuates the importance further by noting that in Leviticus the animal sacrifices are mentioned before any other commandments. He explains that the sacrifices are what "keeps" God amongst us. He recalls a statement of the sages that when the daily Temple sacrifices stopped because of the siege of the city, God "left" the Temple and Jerusalem.

Perhaps it is the offering of something significant. Perhaps it is the offering of a living, breathing being. Perhaps the trauma of the death of an innocent animal should do something to us, to make us realize the seriousness of our encounter with God.

Later, in the Prophets, God states that He doesn't "need" these sacrifices, that the mechanical offering of these beasts without any underlying feeling of remorse, repentance or closeness to God is murder.

How do we get a better understanding of "sacrifice" in our times and what mechanical offerings are we better off not doing?

Dedication
To the Jewish community of Uruguay, their sacrifice on behalf of their brothers. To the shlichim in Montevideo and their self-sacrifice. To Chief Rabbi Lord Jonathan Sacks and his inspiring visit to the community of Uruguay.

Immortal Spirit

"What we do for ourselves dies with us. What we do for others and the world remains and is immortal."- Albert Pine

The Talmud states that the righteous continue to live even after death, while the evil person is considered dead even while he is walking amongst us. The Ohr Hachayim (Leviticus 4:2) explains the metaphysical mechanics of the paradox of the still-living righteous that have passed away versus the live evil personalities that the Talmud labels as dead.

It all has to do with the spirit. The spirit is the immortal component of man that animates his being. However, the spirit is only "alive" if it does good. A spirit that pursues evil shrivels up and eventually "dies." The evil person may be technically alive, but his spirit has long ceased to exist. Hence from a Talmudic point-of-view, the evil person is truly dead.

However, the converse is also true. A spirit that pursues good remains alive long after the body is gone. That spirit remains, and as it is immortal it exists, by definition, forever.

Dedication

To the memory of Tila Tocker, may her memory be blessed, who passed away this Wednesday at the age of 94. She was the mother of Yossi and Sammy Tocker, grandmother of my wife Tamara and her brother Ilan and great-grandmother to our respective children. She was born in Germany and fled the night of the Krystalnacht to Israel. After the establishment of the State of Israel, she and her husband, Jacob Tocker, eventually made their home in Washington Heights, NY. She was an incredible woman and will be greatly missed. Her immortality touches us all.

Tzav

[Leviticus Chapters VI-VIII]

BERESHIT SHEMOT **VAYIKRA** BAMIDBAR DEVARIM   Baal Haturim
Vayikra **Tzav** Shemini Tazria Metzora Acharei Mot Kedoshim Emor Behar Bechukotai

Sinful Ignorance

Ignorance breeds monsters to fill up the vacancies of the soul that are unoccupied by the verities of knowledge. -Horace Mann

"I don't know" is an honest, often acceptable and at times even an admirable response. However, in Jewish law "I don't know" can be criminal.

The overarching command of Jewish law is the self-referential study of the Torah; becoming acquainted with the laws, traditions and customs of what we call the Jewish faith. If you don't know the law, you can't know how to act, what to do, when to do it, when not to do it, and in a system that comprises 248 positive commands and 365 prohibitions, that's a lot of laws we can make mistakes on. We should become familiar with at least the basic ones.

The Baal Haturim on Leviticus 6:1 explains that the Kohanim, the priests of the Temple, were diligent in the fulfillment of their roles and in studying for it. He elaborates further that when there is an error in ones learning and therefore in the performance of a command it is considered in a way a purposeful sin. The person was negligent in their study and that negligence leads directly to the unavoidable mistake.

"I don't know" is no longer an excuse. "I didn't study those laws" does not exempt one from divine judgment. In our day and age, there is absolutely no barrier of access to the entirety of Jewish law, instantaneously, in multiple languages, on multiple sites, apps, books and a plethora of approachable Rabbis worldwide.

We should be constantly educating ourselves.

Dedication

To the TLV Internationals community for hosting us this Shabbat. Looking forward to a memorable event.

Unholy Leftovers

"Gratitude unlocks the fullness of life. It turns what we have into enough, and more. It turns denial into acceptance, chaos to order, confusion to clarity. It can turn a meal into a feast, a house into a home, a stranger into a friend. Gratitude makes sense of our past, brings peace for today, and creates a vision for tomorrow". -Melody Beattie

Disclaimer: I truly enjoy leftovers and look forward to eating as much as I can get of my wife's cooking. The above title is not meant in any way as a negative reflection of her culinary abilities, as our many guests can attest to.

However, in the list of animal sacrifices that were offered at the Sanctuary/Temple there are curious guidelines as to the time span within which the meat can be eaten. For the sacrifice of thanksgiving (Toda) there is an interesting combination of a relatively short period to eat and a lot of bread that is meant to accompany the sacrifice.

The Toda sacrifice is brought when a person wishes to give thanks to God for a particularly significant event, salvation, or overt manifestation of God in ones life.

The Netziv on Leviticus 7:13 explains that the constrained time to eat plentiful food for the thanksgiving offering is deliberate. Its purpose is to force the person to publicize the sacrifice he's offering and the cause, and to invite as many people as possible to partake in the feast of thanks thereby spreading the word far and wide as to God's direct involvement in our lives. Hence, by prohibiting leftovers, one is obliged to invite more people than he might have otherwise.

May we always have reasons to celebrate together and thank God for the goodness and the miraculous in our lives.

Dedication

To all those who know how to have fun without getting drunk.

A Life for a Life

"Behold, I do not give lectures or a little charity. When I give I give myself." -Walt Whitman

How does a person show thanks? How does one repay an enormous debt of gratitude? How can "thank you" be meaningful?

Why, by bringing a sacrifice, of course.

At least that's what they did in the old days. By slaughtering and burning an animal upon the altar one could give thanks to God for saving one from trouble. Ibn Ezra (on Leviticus 7:12) says that a sacrifice was the appropriate method of giving serious thanks. Anything less than that just didn't show enough appreciation to God.

On Leviticus 8:23, he takes the concept of an animal sacrifice another step. The truth is we should be ready to lay our lives on the line for God (when called for). We should be able to give our life in His service. A significant demonstration, beyond mere lip-service was the offering of an animal. A life for a life. The animal being sacrificed was really a substitute for ourselves. It was taking our place on the altar. We needed to imagine, visualize and believe that it is our body being offered. By strongly identifying with the animal and understanding that it is dying instead of us, we can ennoble both its death and our lives.

That is a serious thank you. However, in our days we need to find less destructive and fatal forms of thanks. We have to find some other way to give of ourselves.

Dedication

Thanks to the leadership of both the Kehila of Uruguay as well as the Yavne school community of Montevideo for their extraordinary hosting. Here my thanks are a mere dedication, but I look forward to the opportunity of showing more significant thanks.

BERESHIT SHEMOT **VAYIKRA** BAMIDBAR DEVARIM   *Ohr Hachayim*
Vayikra **Tzav** Shemini Tazria Metzora Acharei Mot Kedoshim Emor Behar Bechukotai

Fragrant Deception

"There is no odor so bad as that which arises from goodness tainted." - Henry David Thoreau

Perfume has probably existed since at least the time of Eve in the Garden of Eden; however it was only in Medieval Europe that it became a permanent fixture of life. During that era, it was widely believed that it was dangerous to ones health to bathe. In order to mask the bodily stench, perfume was increasingly and excessively used by both men and women alike.

(As an aside, it's ironic that at the time Jews were the only population to regularly bathe, which in turn is theorized to have spared them from the worst effects of the Black Plague. This not surprisingly led them to be blamed for the Plague, inspiring further pogroms in a naturally anti-Semitic environment.)

The Ohr Hachayim (near end of Exodus 6:2) has an interesting view on body odor. While modern marketing of fragrances sells us on becoming someone else (typically an exotic impossibly beautified and photoshoped model), the Ohr Hachayim claims that our natural odor actually reflects our true self.

He explains that the righteous emit a sweet fragrance, while evil-doers will have a certain stench. In other words, ones actions leave an olfactory trail that can be picked up by those with sensitive noses.

May we always have a sweet scent – whether natural or artificial.

Dedication

To my brother Boaz, purveyor of fragrance, and to JJ and Elisha Kahen for their wonderful, delicious and fattening hosting.

שמיני

Shemini

[Leviticus Chapters IX-XI]

BERESHIT SHEMOT **VAYIKRA** BAMIDBAR DEVARIM   Baal Haturim
Vayikra Tzav **Shemini** Tazria Metzora Acharei Mot Kedoshim Emor Behar Bechukotai

Bugs in Paradise

We hope that, when the insects take over the world, they will remember with gratitude how we took them along on all our picnics. -Bill Vaughan

The laws of keeping Kosher can at times seem complex and involve much minutia. One can paint in broad strokes the basic laws: no mixing of meat and milk products, kosher mammals must have split hooves and chew their cud, they must be slaughtered and checked according to strict guidelines; kosher fish are only those that have scales and fins, and a few other fundamental guidelines.

However, matters get interesting when we start mixing things, when we deal with modern manufacturing processes, when there are doubts and uncertainty about what exactly we are eating. Then the Rabbis in all their glory attack the subject matter with encyclopedias worth of details, arguments, counter-arguments, decisions and responsa.

One interesting detail is that in some mixtures a rule of thumb is that if there is less than one sixtieth of the offending substance in the mixture (which is not a lot), the entirety of the mixture is permissible to eat. However, a curious exception is bugs. Any food or mixture of food that has even a tiny bug makes that food prohibited.

The Baal Haturim on Leviticus 11:29 adds an unexpected explanation as to why. He writes that snakes are included in the group of insects, bugs and general "creepy crawlies" (sheretz is the exact Hebrew word) that are prohibited. And because the snake is considered so repulsive we can't allow any of it, not even a little bit, no matter how big whatever it's swallowed into is, to be consumed. The snake implicates all other bugs in this prohibition, making life more challenging for all those people checking for bugs in the food we eat, but ostensibly also making it better to eat.

May we stay clear of bugs and snakes in our lives and in our food.

Dedication

To all those who were so careful to avoid chametz (unleavened bread) throughout Pesach.

Scheduling Joy

"Tranquil pleasures last the longest; we are not fitted to bear the burden of great joys." – Nevell Bovee

Weddings are generally happy events. The bride, groom and their families prepare for months, investing great time and money to ensure that every garment, dish, flower, tablecloth and picture will be to their and their guests' liking.

There is joy, dancing and merriment. It is thought to be among the happiest moments of the couple's life. The Netziv on Leviticus 9:1 throws cold water on that concept. He comes to his conclusion from the Jewish experience upon receiving God's law.

When the Jewish people receive the Torah on Mount Sinai, there is fire, lightning, trumpet blasts – a bright and loud show. Only when the Tablets that Moses brought from Sinai are placed in their permanent home, in the Tabernacle, do we see the Jewish nation celebrating and feasting.

The Netziv compares the event at Mount Sinai to the wedding night. There is excitement, perhaps even giddiness, but the bride and groom are too nervous, too anxious to truly experience joy. When the Tablets are placed in the Tabernacle is when the bride and groom come home. Only at home can they truly celebrate. Only at home can they truly experience a serious, tranquil, long-lasting joy.

May joy always be a part of our lives.

Dedication
To those that invest time and money in after the wedding.

BERESHIT SHEMOT **VAYIKRA** BAMIDBAR DEVARIM   *Ibn Ezra*
Vayikra Tzav **Shemini** Tazria Metzora Acharei Mot Kedoshim Emor Behar Bechukotai

"Don't Lecture Me..."

"What you dislike in another take care to correct in yourself." -Thomas Sprat

In Jewish tradition, the High Priest is granted a spectrum of ritual powers and responsibilities. One of the many curious ones is the ability, through animal sacrifice, to beseech for divine atonement for the nation of Israel.

However, before the High Priest brings this powerful sacrifice that has the ability to achieve forgiveness for the multitude of Israel, he is first directed to bring a personal atonement sacrifice.

Ibn Ezra on Leviticus 9:7 explains that the High Priest needs to attain personal redemption first, before he can dare intermediate in the atonement of anyone else. One can't expect a person guilty of a certain sin to be successful in freeing someone else of their spiritual blotch while he is still mired in the same problem. The potential penitent would scoff at such hypocritical preaching.

We need to clean our side of the street before we dare lecture anyone else about theirs.

Dedication

To the various role models who have indeed straightened out their acts and inspire us by example.

BERESHIT SHEMOT **VAYIKRA** BAMIDBAR DEVARIM　　Ohr Hachayim
Vayikra Tzav **Shemini** Tazria Metzora Acharei Mot Kedoshim Emor Behar Bechukotai

Humans in the Zoo

"Man is the Only Animal that Blushes. Or needs to." - Mark Twain

During the intermediate days (Chol Hamoed) of Passover it seems as if every mobile Israeli and tourist leaves their home and invades every road, mall and any available public place in astonishing numbers. I had the opportunity to visit, along with many thousands of others, the "Safari" of Ramat Gan, which proved to be insightful regarding both humans and animals.

Perhaps I have been the victim of too many Disney movies but I perceived (or imagined) a certain intelligence in the eyes of the creatures staring back at me through the fences, glass walls or enclosures that were the prison and homes of the objects of our curiosity. This was in stark contrast to the mindless hordes of humans plodding through the labyrinth of the zoo, moving from watering hole to watering hole, ravenously consuming vast amounts of unleavened products and instinctively herding their young past captured mammals, reptiles and fowl.

Many of the zoo-dwellers were exotic, unfamiliar or just plain frightening to a simple city-dweller. Only the petting-zoo had familiar domesticated animals – mammals of medium size and calm disposition with which I could feel a certain amount of comfort or even closeness – the calf, the sheep, the goat.

The Ohr Hachayim (Leviticus 9:8) claims that our connection to the animal world is more than just taxonomical, especially when we sin. He claims that when we sin, when we do the wrong thing, we are behaving like animals. We are letting our instincts and baser desires rule us and are abandoning the unique human quality of rational self-will. In a sense we become animals.

Therefore, as a remedy for our sin, it is only reasonable that an animal become part of our repentance. An animal is sacrificed. The life of an animal represents our animal selves that sinned and that animal is killed on God's altar. The act of connecting with and then bringing a sacrifice is meant to nullify or at least weaken our animal selves and reaffirm our human aspect, our human nobility, our human free-will and destiny.

May we break free from the zoo of animalistic behaviors and walk tall and proud as proper *Homo sapiens*.

Dedication

To the wider Spitz clan, for an enjoyable, memorable and human-strengthening Pesach. And to the complete and speedy recovery of all the recently injured.

תזריע

Tazria

[Leviticus Chapters XII-XIII]

BERESHIT SHEMOT **VAYIKRA** BAMIDBAR DEVARIM   Baal Haturim
Vayikra Tzav Shemini **Tazria** Metzora Acharei Mot Kedoshim Emor Behar Bechukotai

Animal Tension

Man is the only animal that can remain on friendly terms with the victims he intends to eat until he eats them. -Samuel Butler

There is an internal debate within the Torah as to the treatment of animals. There is an explicit command against cruelty to animals, known in Hebrew as "tzaar baalei chaim" – that we must refrain from causing anguish to animals. However, it is also a given in the Torah that we can eat kosher animals, sacrifice them and use their skins.

So where do we draw the line? The Torah in multiple places provides protection and great sensitivity to animals: you can't muzzle an animal while it's working, you can't overburden the load on an animal, you cannot have two different species pulling a load together, and additional protections. But it seems clear that animals can be used for constructive purposes. They can be harnessed as beasts of burden. They can be killed for digestive, sartorial or ritual purposes.

The Baal Haturim on Leviticus 12:6 gives at the same time what is perhaps the finest delineation of the sensitivity and the uses the Torah assigns to animals.

Amongst the various animal sacrifices that can be brought in the Temple, there are also birds. There are two types of birds that are mentioned: The "Torim" and the "Bnei Yona" (often translated as doves and young pigeons though there is some disagreement as to the exact nomenclature). Most often these bird sacrifices are brought in pairs, and the phrase that is used is "Torim o Bnei Yona", with the "Torim" always before the "Bnei Yona". However, in one instance, where only one bird is sacrificed, the order is reversed.

The Baal Haturim explains that the Torah has an extreme sensitivity to the well-being of the animals. The "Torim" are apparently a lifelong monogamous species and if one of them were to be sacrificed the partner would remain mate-less for life. So in the case of a single bird sacrifice it is preferable to bring from the faithless "Bnei Yona" that will not impact on any avian soul-mates.

May we treat animals with their due respect and understand their acceptable uses.

Dedication

To our sons Akiva and Elchanan who've been taking care of the precious Jerusalem Biblical Zoo and its special residents.

A Secret of Jewish Marriage

"Subdue your appetites, my dears, and you've conquered human nature." -Charles Dickens

There is a commandment that is not spoken about frequently or openly due to its sensitive nature and as a result is also not well known amongst many people. It is the law of Family Purity (taharat ha'mishpacha).

In essence, what it legislates, is that a married couple cannot have any physical contact the days during which the woman experiences her monthly period of menstruation. The couple can only touch again after a suitable period of waiting and after the woman has gone to the ritual bath (mikveh).

This monthly cycle of separation and reunion can have a transformative effect on the couple's relationship and marriage. The Netziv on Leviticus 12:2 explains that this is purposeful. By having a brief period of enforced separation from intimacy each spouse may become more attracted to the other. Besides increasing the physical attraction, it also frames the relationship as not just a physical one but also a spiritual one. It encourages the couple to talk to each other. It inspires the couple to find and do activities together beyond just the physical. Instead of focusing just on our bodies, we also focus on our souls.

Anyone wanting to know more about this important aspect of married Jewish life is invited to contact your local Rabbi or Rebbetzin.

Dedication

To the Mikveh ladies who selflessly assist in this vital commandment.

מצורע

Metzora

[Leviticus Chapters XIV-XV]

Some people never learn...

"Obstinacy is will asserting itself without being able to justify itself. It is persistence without a reasonable motive. It is the tenacity of self-love substituted for that of reason and conscience." -Henri Frederic Amiel

It is said that experience is the best teacher, but sometimes even that is not enough. There are times when actions and their consequences are so clear that it is only by a great force of will or delusion that the correct lessons are ignored.

The Torah dedicates a lot of ink to the malady known as tzaraat. There are three categories of tzaraat: afflictions upon the structure of ones house, afflictions upon ones clothing and affliction upon ones body. Tzaraat is generally attributed to gossip. Rabbinic commentators explain that if one gossips, God sends an initial warning by affecting ones house. The damage, minor as it may be, is meant to be an opportunity to deliberate as to the spiritual ills that lead to the physical harm.

If one gets the message, they clean up their act, fix their house and life goes on. However, the Netziv on Leviticus 14:44 explains, if one doesn't get the message, if one doesn't excise the spiritual illness from themselves, the tzaraat will return and with more force.

The second level that is affected, is ones clothing, ones personal possessions – much closer. The final level that is affected is ones body.

May we use the opportunities that damage and afflictions give us to contemplate our lives and areas for repair and improvement, especially regarding the great evil of gossip.

Dedication

To all those who are both careful with what they put in their mouths over Pesach as well as with what comes out of their mouths the whole year.

Holy Thumbs

According to a decades-old study, 92% of infants suck their thumb. Besides all of the normal physiological reasons, I think I've stumbled upon another reason for a baby's fascination and attachment to that particular finger.

In the Sanctuary (and later in the Temple) there is a ritual performed to purify a recovered "leper", *metzora* in Hebrew, though leper is a poor but common translation of what is considered a spiritual ailment that displays itself physically upon the skin. Part of the ritual was to take the blood of a sacrificed sheep and place it on the right earlobe, right thumb and right big toe of the healed "leper".

Ibn Ezra on Leviticus 14:14 wonders what's so special about the thumb. He then goes on to explain that the thumb is none other than the nexus of the physical and the spiritual. The thumb (think opposable) is what allows man to convert his spiritual desires into concrete action. If it weren't for our (opposable) thumbs, we would be hard pressed to make and wield tools, to write, to craft or to do most things that humans have developed over millennia.

A child sucking his thumb may be doing much more than seeking comfort and pleasure. He may very well be retaining his connection to the spiritual world, seeking the power of the nexus of body and soul, the most physical part of the body that differentiates man from other primates, the most important digit of the hand.

I will never look at a child sucking their thumb the same way again.

Dedication

To my nieces and nephews of thumb-sucking age. May you always retain your connection to the spiritual.

The Sin of Haste

"Truth is confirmed by inspection and delay; falsehood by haste and uncertainty." - Tacitus

The laws of *Tzaraat* (a spiritual skin disease commonly mistranslated as leprosy) are unusual to say the least. *Tzaraat* can afflict a person's body, their clothing or their home. A rule for *Tzaraat* of the house is that a suspected house must be emptied of all its contents before the Kohen arrives for a final inspection and declares his verdict.

The Ohr Hachayim (Leviticus 14:36) wonders why the procedure involves the arduous task of completely emptying ones home, when there is a possibility that the suspected *Tzaraat* house may not be truly infected. Even if the Kohen does decide during the final inspection that the house is indeed afflicted with this spiritual disease, there is still some time, before he leaves the premises and declares the verdict, to remove their belongings.

The Ohr Hachayim explains that the Torah is concerned for the person's possessions. If the *Tzaraat* suspect waits until the last minute and the ruling is that the house is infected he will be rushed to clear his stuff. In his haste he will forget some of his possessions, incurring a loss, as possessions that remain in the house will then be considered contaminated and some of them will not be salvageable.

The Torah prefers that the suspect clear his belongings calmly and without undue time pressure. That way there is a greater likelihood that he will do a more thorough and comprehensive job as opposed to a last-minute whirlwind half-mad effort that is sure to forget important items.

May we know what things to do quickly and which ones to do calmly – and do them.

Dedication

To Yona Benscher on his Bar-Mitzvah. His pace of Torah reading was just right.

אחרי מות

Acharei Mot

[Leviticus Chapters XVI-XVIII]

Smart Diet

"Their kitchen is their shrine, the cook their priest, the table their altar, and their belly their god." -Charles Buck

There is a now-apocryphal story making the rounds of a gentile mother in a supermarket telling her nagging child that he can't have something because it's "not kosher." A curious Jew inquires as to the family's identity. The mother readily admits she is not Jewish, but says she picked up the term watching a Jewish mother in a supermarket in a similar circumstance of a nagging child, and then magically, the words "it's not kosher" immediately stopped all annoying requests. The gentile mother was impressed and now uses the sorcerous word for any situation where she will brook no argument. More TV? "Not kosher", a new toy? "Not kosher". The child may grow up with a skewed understanding of what the term "kosher" means, but there is one underlying meaning that they got. It involves a statement that the item or action is out of bounds. There is a higher authority that has deemed that whatever it is you want, you need to control yourself and accept that not all your desires can be fulfilled.

In the business of eating there is a wide spectrum of practices in regards to observing the laws of eating Kosher. They range from being directly involved in slaughtering, processing and eating only foods where one personally supervised the production, to the other extreme of eating anything that crawls, is grown, found or manufactured on our planet. Within that range there are people who rely only on very specific supervision groups; those that will rely on any Jewish supervision; those that will purchase and prepare Kosher products for the home, but be more lax on what they eat outside; those that are particular that their meat and chicken are kosher but are less concerned about any other products; and an infinite variety of other standards, preferences and personal quirks when it comes to determining what we ingest.

There are also a variety of reasons that are proposed as to why one should eat Kosher. A popular one that receives sporadic scientific support is that it's healthier. A Kabbalistic reason is that it helps the soul. The Netziv on Leviticus on 17:16 gives a reason I hadn't heard before: eating Kosher makes you smarter. He phrases it in the negative. Eating non-kosher makes you dumb. Giving in to ones cravings and baser emotions makes one dumb and can lead a person to other sins. Therefore the reverse must also be true. By eating a kosher diet, it must somehow improve ones intelligence, ones mental capacity and agility. It leads one to restrain oneself, to exhibit self-control. Such mastery can be a strong developer of character and of a sense of boundaries. And it may also be healthier for body and soul.

BERESHIT SHEMOT **VAYIKRA** BAMIDBAR DEVARIM   Netziv
Vayikra Tzav Shemini Tazria Metzora **Acharei Mot** *Kedoshim Emor Behar Bechukotai*

May all who choose to, enjoy a happy and kosher Pesach.

Dedication

To my friend and colleague, Moshe Silberberg, for his unending efforts to provide Kosher food to the Jewish community of Uruguay.

Flawless Transmission

The ability to express an idea is well nigh as important as the idea itself." -Bernard Baruch

One of the more memorable games from kindergarten was 'broken telephone.' At that age I already enjoyed and appreciated how quickly and easily our words can be distorted. To say 'banana' at the beginning of the chain and then to hear 'your Mama' was an insightful lesson in human communications.

Critics of Jewish tradition have often called on this principal to argue against the validity of the Torah, of the Law of Moses, either questioning its divine origin or arguing that there must have been a breakdown or errors in the transmission.

The Ohr Hachayim (Leviticus 16:34) takes a strong stance against such criticism (I guess it was an issue in his time and place as well). At the end of a series of commands performed by Aaron, the High Priest (brother of Moses), the Torah adds a seemingly superfluous line: "and he did as God commanded." The Ohr Hachayim explains that the verse comes to praise both Aaron and Moses. Aaron is praised for having performed all the commands exactly as he had been instructed with no errors whatsoever. However, Aaron did not hear the command straight from God. Moses was the middle-man and he is praised for having transmitted God's words perfectly with "not a sixtieth of a hairsbreadth" difference between God's command and his own recitation.

The Ohr Hachayim states that the entire transmission of the Torah is the same. Moses passed it on flawlessly. There is no error. His contact with God was a clear seamless connection that brought the divine will into human terms and language.

To me it's an amazing realization that the Word of God is right in front of us, in black and white, in the Torah, exactly as He transmitted it. Now if we could only understand what He was telling us…

Dedication

To the iPhone, Skype and modern communications technology. While it is still far from flawless, the connection they enable is highly appreciated

קדושים

Kedoshim

[Leviticus Chapters XIX-XX]

Sinner's Advantage

Many of the insights of the saint stem from their experience as sinners. - Eric Hoffer

A sinner who reaches a level of guilt or even embarrassment over their past failings will often feel inadequate in the presence of those ostensibly better behaved than themselves. They may feel morally inferior, even corrupt in front of those who have not been down the dark roads they've traversed. On a devoutness scale, they may always fall short. They may wonder what they can contribute to the world when there are people in it who are so much better than they are.

The Baal Haturim on Leviticus 20:3 states a principle of faith that turns the above calculation on its head and echoes the Talmudic dictum that "in the place/level that a repentant sinner stands, a completely righteous man cannot stand/reach."

The Baal Haturim gives more detail to this evocative statement. He claims that when a sinner repents of his sins, somehow, through some divine transmutation, those sins are converted into merits. So if we were to attempt to illustrate the concept mathematically, let us imagine a sinner who is on a divine obedience level of let's say -10. His friend, the wonderfully righteous man who hasn't sinned has an impressive +6, 16 levels above our friend the sinner. Should the sinner truly and deeply repent, his level is transformed from a -10 to a +10, surpassing our righteous friend who hasn't tasted sin.

There is something truly powerful and valuable about a person who realizes his mistake, regrets it and in a significant fashion turns himself around. This is a tremendously greater challenge than for the person who has not had and has not lived through the same temptations and trials, who is not used to certain behavior or actions. Perhaps where we see the repentant man's sins used positively (of course this is not an excuse to sin...) is when he uses his unique capacity to assist others with the same background and challenges. The righteous may have a theoretical understanding of the issues, but can rarely reach the level of interaction, communication and effectiveness of the repentant sinner.

May we sinners understand our true value and capacity for good – and fulfill it.

Dedication

To the IDF soldiers assisting the earthquake victims in Nepal. You are an inspiration.

Religious Convenience

"The ultimate measure of a man is not where he stands in moments of comfort and convenience, but where he stands at times of challenge and controversy." -Martin Luther King, Jr.

There is a trend in religious life, whether one was born into it, or one joins it later in life, to live a certain lifestyle, within a certain community. Aspects of religious service become rote. We do things without giving it much thought. It becomes convenient. If we are confronted with a change from the comfortable, if there is something in the religious obligation that we don't like or inconveniences us, then we decide that we are doing enough in our divine obligations, that there is no need to be "so" religious.

In a related theme, there is an unusual and particularly harsh punishment concerning eating of sacrificial meat that was offered during Temple times. It is meant to be consumed within two days. If it is eaten on the third day – a sin known as "pigul", the violator's punishment is "karet", which is translated as "cut off". "Karet" is variably explained as he will die young, his children will die, and/or his eternal soul will cease to be. However one looks at it, it seems like an inordinately unforgiving penalty for what amounts to eating leftovers a day past their expiration date.

The Netziv on Leviticus 19:8 explains that the infraction reveals a much deeper problem. If one eats within the prescribed time, then all is well. However, if one decides that it is not convenient, that he wishes to indulge a bit more in the tasty and expensive meat that he already paid for and grilled, then it demonstrates that his entire service of God is really self-serving. His lifestyle is in reality one of indulgence and gratification and is an express rejection of and rebellion against God. Such a person though outwardly "observant" has issues with his understanding of the demands and responsibilities of divine service.

May we strengthen the good things we do and do them because they are right, and not just convenient.

Dedication

To all those who exerted themselves in preparing and providing Kosher for Passover food. It certainly wasn't convenient, but was highly delicious and appreciated.

With great power...

"He who is false to present duty breaks a thread in the loom, and will find the flaw when he may have forgotten its cause." -Henry Ward Beecher

In the fabricated mythology of our modern era, perhaps one character stands alone as the epitome of responsibility. I am talking, of course, of Marvel Comics' angst-ridden, smart-mouthed, arachnid-powered Spider-Man.

In the story of his genesis, the super-powered youth hailing from Forest Hills, NY, (my neighborhood!), uses his newfound abilities exclusively for fame and glory. He witnesses an armed robbery, and in his egocentric blasé, allows the thief to escape, though he could have easily stopped him. However, fate is not kind to the unhelpful bystander. The same thief later accosts and kills Spider-Man's beloved uncle and guardian, Uncle Ben.

Awakened harshly and directly to the consequences of his inaction, Spider-Man vows to dedicate his life to fighting injustice, living by his dead uncle's motto, which Marvel has made so famous: "With great power, comes great responsibility."

Ibn Ezra is of the opinion that Spider-Man's self-blame is well placed. In Leviticus 19:11 he explains the unusual usage of the plural form in the commandment of not to steal. He explains that it means to include not only the direct perpetrator of a crime, but also those that stand by quietly and do nothing when they could have. They are equally guilty of the crime.

Spider-Man took the lesson to heart. May we never stand by idly when duty calls.

Dedication

To the fictional Parker family (Peter/Spider-Man, Uncle Ben and Aunt May). They were entertaining role models.

אֱמֹר

Emor

[Leviticus Chapters XXI-XXIV]

BERESHIT SHEMOT **VAYIKRA** BAMIDBAR DEVARIM   Baal Haturim
Vayikra Tzav Shemini Tazria Metzora Acharei Mot Kedoshim **Emor** Behar Bechukotai

The Sin of Missed Opportunities

Four things come not back. The spoken word, the sped arrow, the past life, and the neglected opportunity. -Arabic Proverb

Jewish faith is defined, constrained and guided by a set of rules. Commandments direct how we should act, speak and even think. Jewish law (Halacha) in all of its complexity and subtlety is meant to be a guidebook for life.

To a person that is just becoming familiar with the plethora of laws, the extensiveness and detail of the commandments can be overwhelming. However, there are a number of overarching principles that can assist and that are worth keeping in mind:

- Continuous Torah study is fundamental – if you don't know, you can't do.
- Don't do unto others what you wouldn't like to be done to you.
- The Sabbath is a key mainstay of the Jewish people.
- Idol worship is a fundamental negation of Jewish faith.

There are a few others, but one that Baal Haturim relates to is chosen by one of the most authoritative redactors of Jewish Law, Rabbi Yosef Karo, to start off his magnum opus, the Shulchan Aruch.

The Baal Haturim on Leviticus 22:29 warns us not to let the opportunity to perform a Mitzvah (a commandment) pass us by. The chance to fulfill a precept of Jewish law is often fleeting and once lost is gone forever. We are enjoined to be swift in the pursuit of God's directives. We must awaken with alacrity to use our time, our resources, our intelligence, and our strengths to lead a life that seizes upon the opportunities that are in front of us.

May we always grasp the opportunities to do good.

Dedication

To the team of Merkaz HaHalacha (Center of Jewish Law) who continue to grow and succeed.

Selective Lineage

"From our ancestors come our names from our virtues our honor." – Proverb

According to Jewish Law, Jewishness is passed on by ones mother. However, ones tribal affiliation (meaning, of the twelve original tribes of Israel) was passed on by ones father. This remains true in the two major groups within Judaism that still retain a tribal (and sub-tribal) identity – the Levites and the Cohanim.

Therefore, what we would consider the overarching national Jewish identity is a function of matrilineal descent. Meanwhile, the more specific tribal identity is a function of patrilineal descent, though currently less relevant to most Jews, as our tribal histories and lineages have been mostly forgotten in the mists of time. Most non-Levites and non-Cohanim are presumed to descend from some amalgamation of the tribes of Judah and Benjamin. This is not taking into account rediscovered lost tribes, such as Jewish Ethiopians who are believed to be descendants of the tribe of Dan, or Jewish Indians from the tribe of Menashe, or other groups around the world that are being discovered.

However, the Netziv on Leviticus 22:11, highlights yet another, third type of ancestry. Let's call it "sanctity lineage". The case is of a non-Jewish slave woman that was purchased by a Cohen. In a sense the slave is considered the property of the Cohen. A child born to that woman (and not even sired by the Cohen) is likewise considered the property of the Cohen, with the unique and unusual privilege, not available to any other group within Judaism — even though this child is not Jewish — to eat and partake of the "truma", the special portion that Jews in Temple times were required to give to the Cohen and was considered sacred.

What this sheds light on, is that inherited status depends on the purpose. For determining Jewishness, we follow the mother. For determining tribe, we follow the father. For determining whether one can eat from the sacred "truma", we follow the "owner".

May we have clarity on our pedigree, identities and affiliation and know the difference between them.

Dedication

To my friend, Elli Fischer, for his extensive writings in general and his recent article on the difference between identity and affiliation in particular.

Repetitive Repetitions

"The mantram becomes one's staff of life and carries one through every ordeal. Each repetition has a new meaning, carrying you nearer and nearer to God." -Mahatma Gandhi

Since the invention of literary critics, (which came about on the very heels of the invention of authors), there has been much ink spilled complaining about repetition in ones writing. Perhaps the reader sees it as a direct attack on their intellect. "We got it the first time," they must think.

The Bible is replete with repetitions. Perhaps one of the most common phrases that one sees over and over again, (besides "And God spoke to Moses, saying…"), is "I am God" that punctuates a plethora of diverse and unrelated commandments.

I think to myself and say to Him: "Um, with all due respect God, we know You are God. We didn't think it was anybody else. We don't suspect You of having an identity crisis, so what's with the constant deluge of "I am God" throughout Your book?"

Ibn Ezra on Leviticus 22:33 comes to the rescue. He explains that "I am God" takes us back to the First Commandment of the famed Ten. The First Commandment is where God sets the foundation of our belief system. "You must believe in Me." If we don't have the basic belief in God, then the other commandments lack force or meaning. "I am God" is the reason we do the commandments. That is why He needs to accentuate many commandments with this reminder. That is why He punctuates various commands to link the performance of His will with the intrinsic belief in Him. We can never forget that "He is God." It bears repeating. Constantly.

Despite literary and biblical critics, some things are worth hearing over and over and over.

Dedication
To all the teachers who took the pains to repeat themselves.

The Value of the Unneeded

"The true measure of a man is how he treats someone who can do him absolutely no good." -Ann Landers

A new tactic in my arsenal of Aliyah discussions is to state that Israel no longer needs its Jewish masses from the Diaspora. From a military, economic, cultural and demographic perspective Israel is blessed with a healthy, productive, educated population with no critical personnel needs that cannot be fulfilled locally.

This does not contradict the value and the benefit to the individual or family that chooses to join the Jewish people in its homeland. Nonetheless, the tactic of guilt, of implying that a person's presence in Israel is critical to the physical needs and success of the country seems disingenuous to me.

The Ohr Hachayim (Leviticus 21:8) however, does not let people off the hook merely because they are not needed. Individual obligations are still in force even if communal needs have been satisfied. He draws his proof from the sanctity required of a Kohen. The main function of the Kohen was to work in the Temple and to do that work he had to be in a state of sanctity. One might think that as soon as there were enough Kohens to perform the Temple work the requirement for sanctification of the unneeded Kohen would lapse.

That is not true. Even the unneeded Kohen has an obligation to sanctify himself. Even if there is a quorum of ten men, there is still an obligation to pray with a Minyan. Even if the State of Israel has not identified a need for you, there is still a commandment for Jews to live in Israel. The question is not only what can you do for your country or your people. The question is what must you do for yourself.

Dedication

To the Young Israel of Woodmere, now considered the largest Young Israel around. They have understood that the strength of a community is not necessarily for all its members to pray in the same room at the same time. They have found a way for its members to fulfill their individual obligations from a selection of more customized communal venues. I think that makes for a stronger community.

בהר

Behar

[Leviticus Chapters XXV-XXVI]

BERESHIT SHEMOT **VAYIKRA** BAMIDBAR DEVARIM   Baal Haturim
Vayikra Tzav Shemini Tazria Metzora Acharei Mot Kedoshim Emor **Behar** *Bechukotai*

Beneficial Obedience
The ship that will not obey the helm will have to obey the rocks. -English Proverb

God gives the law. The expectation is that we will follow it. But He knows us well. He knows we are a stiff-necked people. He knows that we easily give in to our more basic desires. He knows that wealth, power and comfort corrupt us. He knows that poverty, helplessness and distress weaken us. Nonetheless, we are commanded. We are enjoined to obey.

There are a plethora of blessings that are listed for those that follow God's commandments, just as there is a long list of curses for those that ignore God's directives.

The Baal Haturim on Leviticus 25:11 highlights a particular facet of obedience. He claims that being obedient assures one that their lineage will continue. There is something about following God's orders that instills in God a desire to see future generations of such people. On the other hand, the punishment for the disobedient is exile. The disobedient will not be able to enjoy life at home. They will be exiled. They will have to wander the earth, separated from their roots.

May we pay attention to what God wants of us and merit a long lineage in our homeland.

Dedication
To the new government of Israel.

Family Reconciliation

"So much of what is best in us is bound up in our love of family, that it remains the measure of our stability because it measures our sense of loyalty. All other pacts of love or fear derive from it and are modeled upon it." -Haniel Long

Fights within families are part of human nature. Spouses; children with their parents; siblings – all have their share of altercations. However, sometimes some disagreements are so vitriolic, so hard fought, so anger-inducing that a separation ensues. The separation may be short-lived and the family members reconcile, reunite and family life continues. But other times, the damage is so deep, so hurtful, that only time and distance seems to ease the pain.

The Torah mandates that every fifty years the properties within the land of Israel must revert to their original owners. It is the Jubilee year that is celebrated at the end of a cycle of seven Sabbatical years. The Netziv on Leviticus 25:10 notes that the verse of the Jubilee uses a dual language. It states that each person will return to his inheritance *and* to his family.

The Netziv explains that this verse is speaking to family members who have grown distant, who have left their ancestors home, who may have differences, who may have traveled to distant lands and foreign shores. It is stating that the Jubilee is an opportunity to return home, to reconcile, to return to ones roots. Not only is it an opportunity, not only is it a right and a privilege – it is an obligation.

May we not have to wait for the Jubilee to return to our proper homes.

Dedication

To the State of Israel on its 66th birthday and to its Uruguayan emissaries. It's wonderful to celebrate our homeland's growth and success together.

Beware the Jealous

"The thermometer of success is merely the jealousy of the malcontents."
-Salvador Dali

Since the beginning of the modern State of Israel our neighbors have continuously tried to kill us. More than a century ago Jewish pioneers came to a land of swamps and deserts and with back-breaking sacrifice created a modern miracle of terraforming.

Arabs were soon attracted to the newly habitable fertile land and have been a fairly harmful presence ever since. What has ensued is an interminable war, both from within and from outside our borders, with ebbs and flows dictated by politicians and secured by Israel's Defense Forces.

Despite terror, despite embargoes, despite boycotts, Israel continues to grow and flourish to the chagrin, dismay and embarrassment of its neighbors. Will there ever be a time of peace? Will there ever be a time that we can sit in our land unafraid of attack, unafraid of the jealousy and hatred of those around us?

The Ohr Hachayim says "Yes!" He talks lovingly of the land of Israel. He wonders at a curious repetition of the term "secure" in the Bible (Leviticus 25:19). He then explains that it is a prophecy of future days. God is promising that in that future date, when our land will blossom and give forth fruit, our borders will become secure. We will not fear any attack. However, not only will our land be secure, but even our produce will be safe from jealous thieves, maddened by our success and accomplishment.

May we break free from the corrosive affects of jealousy and may it happen speedily in our day.

Dedication

To Israel's farmers – the producers of the best crops in the world.

בחוקתי

Bechukotai

[Leviticus Chapters XXVI-XXXIV]

Self-punishment

"A human being fashions his consequences as surely as he fashions his goods or his dwelling. Nothing that he says, thinks or does is without consequences." -Norman Cousins

The Torah is as harsh with its punishments as it is generous with its rewards. Some people, while happy to receive rewards for good acts, believe it unjust for us to be punished for going against the directives of God.

The Netziv on Leviticus 26:3 explains that God's list of punishments shouldn't be seen as capricious intervention on His part against those who ignore Him. Rather it is a list of warnings, much like a doctor's health warning, that if a person chooses to follow an unhealthy path, then the inevitable consequence is the pain and suffering that will ensue.

The "punishments" then are not necessarily some special response on God's part, but rather it is the natural result of the actions we take. God is merely warning us to avoid such paths in order to be spared from the resultant outcome.

So for our own selfish interest and self-preservation, there may be some wisdom in following God's directives.

Dedication

To the good Rabbis of Buenos Aires for such a warm welcome.

Hellfire-Proof
"Hell is truth seen too late, duty neglected in its season." -Tryon Edwards

The text of the Torah doesn't deal much with the idea of an afterlife. It is focused on the here and now. Rewards and punishments are described in very concrete, physical and material terms.

On the other hand, descriptions of the spiritual realm and the afterlife are part of the Oral Tradition and are expanded upon greatly by sages and Rabbis for millennia. There seems to be widespread agreement that there is some aspect of the afterlife (hell, purgatory, take your pick) that is the physical equivalent to being burned alive.

The Ohr Hachayim (Leviticus 26:16) finds hints to otherworldly punishments in the biblical text. He claims that besides the fiery doom, there is an obstruction of "vision" (whatever that means in the afterlife) and a concomitant wretchedness. However, the text also provides the means of protection from the flames of hell as well as from the other punishments.

The protection is unsurprisingly simple: The Torah. The Ohr Hachayim promises that the flames of Torah study are greater in strength than the flames of hell and will protect its students. Furthermore, the study of Torah "brightens" the eye and will clear any obstructions of vision in the netherworld and finally, knowledge of the Torah is joyous and will dispel any future misery.

Fire-proof, bright-eyed and happy – sounds good to me.

Dedication
To Tracy Chevalier (Girl with a Pearl Earring) and Tom Rob Smith (Child 44), two incredible writers and gracious authors who I had the great pleasure of meeting this week at the International Writer's Festival in Jerusalem.

במדבר

Bamidbar

[Numbers Chapters I-IV]

BERESHIT SHEMOT VAYIKRA **BAMIDBAR** DEVARIM — Baal Haturim
Bamidbar Naso Behaalotcha Shelach Korach Chukat Balak Pinchas Matot Masai

Deathless Future

I don't want to achieve immortality through my work. I want to achieve it through not dying. -Woody Allen

Western man is allergic to death. We try to avoid it, escape it, ignore it. We don't want it mentioned. If we close our eyes, perhaps it won't notice us. The counterpoint to death-avoidance is the desire to want to live forever. To be forever young.

Interestingly, the Torah also has a death-avoidance culture, but one that translates into ritual "impurity" if one is in contact with death, and which subsequently can be "purified". Within the Jewish people, there is a subgroup that is commanded as a whole to avoid death. They are the Kohanim, the priestly descendents of Aharon, the original High Priest (Kohen Gadol).

While death is a fact of life, there are some hints that it is not necessarily a permanent arrangement.

In describing the work that the sons of Aharon, the Kohanim, must do in the Tabernacle, the Torah ends the description with the warning, that if they follow the rules, "they will live and they will not die."

Why the redundancy? It would seem obvious that if someone is going to live they will not die.

The Baal Haturim explains that this is a prophetic hint. On the verse in Numbers 4:19 he details that at some future date, in some eschatological reality, the very Angel of Death will be annulled. Death will have no more sway over humanity.

Humans, or whatever we will be in that future (disembodied souls?) will indeed somehow live forever.

May we be beings worthy of eternal life.

Dedication

To our departed loved ones, who we believe we will be reunited with in some future reality.

Overqualified

"Few men during their lifetime come anywhere near exhausting the resources dwelling within them. There are deep wells of strength that are never used." -Richard E. Byrd

The beginning of the Book of Numbers reintroduces us to Aaron the High Priest and to his sons. His two eldest, Nadav and Avihu, we are reminded, died while bringing the unauthorized "strange" fire during the consecration of the Tabernacle, where they were immediately struck by divine fire.

Aaron's two remaining sons, Elazar and Itamar, are introduced with an unusual phraseology, *"and they served as priests, Elazar and Itamar, over the face of Aaron their father."*

The Netziv on the verse (Numbers 3:4) explains that by mentioning Elazar and Itamar in this fashion, the Torah is telling us that in fact, these two sons were already at a high enough level of sanctity and devotion that they were each worthy of serving as High Priest. However, Elazar needs to wait almost forty years to take over his father's role and we have no account of Itamar, the youngest son, ever filling that prestigious position, even though he was qualified. Instead, we see Itamar having secondary managerial roles in the Tabernacle, always in the shadow of his illustrious father and his more honored older brother – though Itamar is not any less qualified for the important tasks.

Each person has hidden strengths, talents and potential that their current circumstances don't give them the freedom to develop or use. That does not diminish the individual, nor are they free to ignore such attributes. One must seek where they can best use their strengths for the tasks at hand.

May we have opportunities to use as much of our potential as possible.

Dedication

To the upcoming Hebrew Studies teachers of Integral whom I've had the great privilege of teaching. May they fulfill their teaching potential and pass on our heritage to many students.

BERESHIT SHEMOT VAYIKRA **BAMIDBAR** DEVARIM   Ibn Ezra
Bamidbar Naso Behaalotcha Shelach Korach Chukat Balak Pinchas Matot Masai

Lions of Israel

"True courage is a result of reasoning. A brave mind is always impregnable." -Jeremy Collier

There are multiple accounts of the miracles of the Six Day War, when in the summer of 1967, against all odds, Israel not only survived, but prevailed over the Arab countries that had vowed to eradicate our homeland.

My father, then an American student, was one of a handful of volunteers that boarded a plane and contributed to the war effort. This was just two months before his scheduled wedding day, and despite protests and concerns of his family and bride he entered the war zone.

Though he was stationed in a rearguard position, he was spared from any fighting due to the surprising turns of the war.

Ibn Ezra on Numbers 1:19 equates an army's frontline with the rearguard, from our ancestors in the desert:

"Know that there were no tribes as brave as the tribe of Judah who was compared to a lion, and the tribe of Dan, who was likewise compared (to a lion) by Moses, and therefore they were positioned in the front and in the back (of the army of Israel)."

May we ever have lions to inspire us and give us courage to undertake risky adventures for the sake of our brothers.

Dedication

To my father, Elliot Spitz, and to all the soldiers of Israel and for the miracle of regaining our ancient capital after millennia which we celebrated yesterday, Jerusalem Day.

BERESHIT SHEMOT VAYIKRA **BAMIDBAR** DEVARIM Ohr Hachayim
Bamidbar Naso Behaalotcha Shelach Korach Chukat Balak Pinchas Matot Masai

Jewish Warriors

"Conscription may have been good for the country, but it damn near killed the army." -Sir Richard Hull

The first documented record of conscription, of obligating the entire male population of a nation, of a certain age, to serve in its military goes back almost 4,000 years ago in Babylon to the time of Hammurabi (1791-1750 BCE). 600 years later, the fledgling Israelite nation instituted conscription upon its exodus from Egypt. Centuries after that, the Chinese, Greeks and Romans would use conscription.

In European medieval times the custom became one person per family, though it was typically for one to three months, as the feudal lords preferred having their people on the farms for harvest time. In the Middle East, military slavery was developed, starting with the Mamluks in the 9th century until the Ottomans in the 19th century.

After the Renaissance, Europe saw the development of small professional armies. These were fairly effective until the French Revolution and the modern re-introduction of universal conscription. Napoleon Bonaparte was able to overwhelm the professional soldiers of his enemies with a force of conscripts that at times outnumbered his foes ten to one. Other countries have figured it out since (thanks to Wikipedia for most of the above).

One of the problems with conscription is that not all of ones conscripts are suitable soldier material. This has been a predicament for every military leader, whether Sargon, Alexander, Caesar, Hannibal, Ghengis Khan, Stalin or Mao Zedong. All except two military leaders in world history suffered from unqualified conscripts: Moses and Joshua.

In the beginning of the Book of Numbers, Moses lists the number of troops from each Tribe (except the Levites who served in the Chaplaincy, if you will). Before stating the number, Moses continuously adds the phrase **"everyone** who goes out to the legion." According to the Ohr Hachayim (Numbers 1:20) every single male Israelite, from the age of 20 until 60 was a formidable and worthy soldier.

The Ohr Hachayim acknowledges the miraculous phenomena, but this may help explain the lightning-fast victories the Israelites achieved under the leadership of Moses (he conquered a significant portion of modern-day Jordan in just a few months, against mighty kingdoms that caused the Canaanite kings to quiver) and then under Joshua who conquered 31 kingdoms of Canaan (more like fortified cities, but impressive nonetheless) in seven years.

BERESHIT SHEMOT VAYIKRA **BAMIDBAR** DEVARIM Ohr Hachayim
Bamidbar Naso Behaalotcha Shelach Korach Chukat Balak Pinchas Matot Masai

May our current soldiers be as worthy, formidable and successful as our warrior ancestors.

Dedication

To those choosing to serve in the IDF. Though there is formally conscription, it is becoming a self-selecting force.

נשא

Naso

[Numbers Chapters IV-VII]

BERESHIT SHEMOT VAYIKRA **BAMIDBAR** DEVARIM   Baal Haturim
Bamidbar **Naso** Behaalotcha Shelach Korach Chukat Balak Pinchas Matot Masai

Impure Prophecies

It is not the cares of today, but the cares of tomorrow that weigh a man down. For the needs of today we have corresponding strength given. For the morrow we are told to trust. It is not ours yet. -George Macdonald

There is a special, self-chosen condition, that a person during biblical or temple times could elect for themselves. That condition is known as Nazir or Nazarite. There were three requirements for the Nazir: not consuming anything derived from grapes, not cutting their hair and not coming into contact with the dead.

A person chose to become a Nazir as a way to reach greater levels of holiness and become closer to God. At the end of the Nazir period, they would cut their hair and bring sacrifices in the Temple. During the heightened state of sanctity of the Nazir, it was apparently easier for them to feel the divine presence in their lives and perhaps even reach some minor levels of prophecy.

The Baal Haturim on Numbers 6:6 mentions an interesting reason why the Nazir had to avoid the dead during this period. He explains that in the case where the divine presence would rest upon the Nazir, were he to receive some prophetic vision, we don't want anyone to assume or speculate that he might have consulted the dead for his otherworldly insights.

May we stick to pure and divine sources of information.

Dedication

To Jacky Catan and Joel Felder on their upcoming wedding and a future filled will blessings.

Nearby Exile

"Only solitary men know the full joys of friendship. Others have their family; but to a solitary and an exile, his friends are everything." -Willa Cather

Solitary confinement is known as one of the harshest punishments prisoners are given. There is something in being alone for too long that is of greater anguish than physical pain. However, being alone is not only a function of physical separation. There is a social exclusion that can be just as damaging, if not more so, than being the sole occupant of a cell.

For a person that became ritually impure during the sojourn of the tribes of Israel in the desert, the prescription was a temporary exile from the camp. The Netziv on Numbers 5:4 warns however, that when the unfortunate person was exiled, they needed to make sure they did not stray too far away.

The simplest reason is for physical protection. Being outside, yet in close proximity to the camp, afforded some shelter from external forces that may seek to harm the isolated member of the group. For an outsider, from a distance, it would be hard to distinguish the exiled from the tribe.

However, there is a more practical reason. Remaining close, even while in exile, makes it easier to return.

May we keep ourselves and those we have exiled from our lives within reach of the core of our tribe.

Dedication

To Rabbi Eliyahu Birnbaum, former Chief Rabbi of Uruguay, for a wonderful and meaningful visit to his old community.

Suffering's Reward

"Although the world is full of suffering, it is full also of the overcoming of it." – Helen Keller

The Torah makes a straightforward connection between doing good and receiving God's reward and blessing, and doing bad and receiving divine punishment and suffering. Only a few thousand years later do we see rabbinic literature deal with more theologically challenging concepts of sinners who receive reward and righteous who are punished.

Ibn Ezra jumps into this discussion with yet another possibility in the divine ledger-keeping and that is reward as compensation for suffering.

Amongst the strangest rituals described in the Bible is that of the Sotah. It is the process whereby a woman suspected of adultery, who denies any wrongdoing, is publicly degraded and forced to drink a unique concoction called the "bitter waters". During the times of the Sanctuary and the Temple these bitter waters apparently had the power to determine a woman's infidelity. If the woman had been untrue, the waters would cause her to die a gruesome death including the rapid swelling of her stomach and the falling off of body parts. However, if she was innocent, the result would be the birth of a healthy baby boy.

Ibn Ezra on Numbers 5:28 suggests that the resultant birth of a child is a gift, a reward from God to the mother for the blameless suffering she was subjected to. Her being accused by her husband of adultery and the subsequent public degradation despite her repeated, vehement and true affirmations of innocence need to be compensated.

This is when God steps in and rewards the mother with one of the most precious gifts possible: a healthy child.

May all our sufferings lead to sweet rewards.

Dedication

To Rabbi Menachem Burstein (originally from Uruguay) and Machon Puah who helps so many families achieve the special gift of a child.

And Mazal Tov to my colleagues in Montevideo, Rabbi Eliyahu and Natalie Galil on the birth of their fourth child!

BERESHIT   SHEMOT   VAYIKRA   **BAMIDBAR**   DEVARIM   Ohr Hachayim
Bamidbar **Naso** Behaalotcha Shelach Korach Chukat Balak Pinchas Matot Masai

Humble Hero

"Courage and perseverance have a magical talisman, before which difficulties disappear and obstacles vanish into air." -John Quincy Adams

In Jewish mythology, there is one story and one personality that serve as the epitome of bravery. Though it is not in the text of the Bible, a famous Midrash states that Nachshon son of Aminadav, from those exiting Egypt, stood with Moses and the Children of Israel at the Reed Sea, with the Egyptian army fast approaching.

God tells Israel "go into the water." The Midrash explains that Nachshon, filled with faith, was the first and only person to jump into the sea. The water reaches Nachshon's neck and then miraculously parts, allowing the Children of Israel to cross the sea without getting wet.

Nachshon's impetuousness is credited with getting the sea to split. Nachshon is mentioned in the biblical text later as the Prince of the Tribe of Judah and the first of the twelve princes to bring the consecration sacrifice for the brand-new Tabernacle.

The Ohr Hachayim (Numbers 7:12) explores what made Nachshon so great. He notes that from the list of princes, Nachshon is the only one without the title "Prince." He explains that this attests to his humility as well as his greatness. Nachshon's character was so great that he needed no title for it to be recognized. It was his combination of strong faith and great humility that engendered his extraordinary bravery and his leadership position.

May we learn from Nachshon. Sometimes you have to just jump in the water.

Dedication

To all those jumping into the water of Israeli life. Some of the incredible accomplishments and highlights of Israel have been recently documented in a fantastic movie you must see at: http://www.stepupforisrael.com

Mazal Tov to Shaltiel Shmidman on his Bar-Mitzvah and his impressive cantillation of the entire book of Psalms from a scroll.

בהעלותך

Behaalotcha

[Numbers Chapters VIII-XII]

A Father's Blessing

Blessed indeed is the man who hears many gentle voices call him father! -Lydia Maria Child

The Children of Israel had no sooner started their desert journey when they start complaining. Moses, fed up with the growing irritation cries out to God, asking rhetorically that if he gave birth to these stubborn people does it give him the obligation to care for their every need and whim?

Moses is so despondent by the burden of the people of Israel that in his despair he actually asks God to kill him. God helps Moses by both providing meat to the insatiable Israelites as well as directing Moses to gather seventy elders to assist in the burden of leadership.

While on the theme of birth and sons, the Baal Haturim on 11:12 takes the opportunity to relate some of the characteristics that a father normally transmits to his sons. He names five:

1. Looks/appearance
2. Strength
3. Wealth
4. Wisdom
5. Longevity

When these characteristics are good and passed down to children, fathers can take some measure of pride, and children some measure of gratitude. When the characteristics are poor, fathers can feel some guilt and children can assign blame.

However, neither pride nor guilt, gratitude or blame will help us make the most of the gifts we possess.

Dedication

To Bar-Ilan University, training grounds for many fathers and sons.

The Final Battle

"Men are at war with each other because each man is at war with himself." -Francis Meehan

Armed conflict has been a part of history since the birth of brothers. Any differences, be it of ideology, territory or possessions has too often led to war between peoples and groups. When cursing the people of Israel for disobedience, God declares that the Jewish people will lose their wars, as we witnessed 2,000 years ago and before.

However, when God blesses the Jewish nation, He promises that they will win their battles. But there is another statement – they need not fear future battles.

The Netziv on Numbers 10:9 explains that this can only be referring to the final battle at the prophesied "end of days", known in Hebrew as the battle of Gog u'Magog. That will be the battle to end all battles and will usher in an era of everlasting peace. But the Netziv expands that this final battle will only end when people resolve the conflicts within their own beings and specifically when they believe in and accept God in their lives.

May we find ways to resolve our internal battles and be spared the travails of the external ones.

Dedication

To our son, Eitan, on his acceptance to the Israeli Navy. We hope he will spend more time fishing than fighting.

BERESHIT   SHEMOT   VAYIKRA   **BAMIDBAR**   DEVARIM   Ibn Ezra
Bamidbar Naso **Behaalotcha** Shelach Korach Chukat Balak Pinchas Matot Masai

Infinite Light-givers

"We must view young people not as empty bottles to be filled, but as candles to be lit." -Robert H. Shaffer

It is perhaps one of the least noted but most dramatic scenes in the life of Moses. The people of Israel protest and rebel yet again. Their foray into the desert is filled with anger and disappointment. Moses feels that he can no longer lead the tribes of Israel. In an all too human show of despair Moses asks God to strike him dead. He can no longer bear the intense burden of leadership.

God hears Moses' plea and arrives at a solution to allow Moses to share some of the rigors of both prophecy and leadership. Seventy elders are gathered and some of the divine spirit that Moses carried is given to each of the elders, giving them their own prophetic capabilities.

One might assume that Moses would be somewhat diminished by sharing his powers, that his light would not shine as brightly. Ibn Ezra on Numbers 11:17 argues the reverse. He explains that the prophetic spirit is akin to wisdom or to the light of a candle. It is not lessened by sharing. It spreads and the sharer retains all of his prophetic power, all of his wisdom, all of his light.

May we have good things to share and may we share those good things widely.

Dedication

To Marcello Farias of Innuy who is sharing his unique programming talent with the Rabbinate of Uruguay and thereby spreading knowledge of kosher products to more people.

BERESHIT SHEMOT VAYIKRA **BAMIDBAR** DEVARIM Ohr Hachayim
Bamidbar Naso **Behaalotcha** Shelach Korach Chukat Balak Pinchas Matot Masai

The Travel Imperative

"Travel is fatal to prejudice, bigotry, and narrow-mindedness, and many of our people need it sorely on these accounts. Broad, wholesome, charitable views of men and things cannot be acquired by vegetating in one little corner of the earth all one's lifetime." -Mark Twain

I like traveling. I like meeting new people and seeing new places. I like getting a different perspective of the world and widening my horizons. What I didn't realize is that traveling apparently fulfills a spiritual requirement.

There is a Kabbalistic concept of "sparks" strewn about our planet. These sparks are everywhere and in order to fulfill our ultimate destiny, humanity must unlock and collect these sparks (whatever that means). To complicate matters further, there are sparks that can only be released by specific people at specific times in specific places.

The Ohr Hachayim (Numbers 10:35) explains that there are different levels of sparks and these sparks may require different amounts of time to access. For some sparks it's just enough to pass by (reaching some realization?) while other sparks need a longer presence (affecting some change at the place?).

Whatever the task, there are some sparks that need to be dealt with on the road or outside of the house and we might as well enjoy this spiritual need and imperative to travel and interact with the wider world.

Dedication

To all of the people who have made our travels possible and memorable.

שלח

Shelach

[Numbers Chapters XIII-XV]

BERESHIT SHEMOT VAYIKRA **BAMIDBAR** DEVARIM   Baal Haturim
Bamidbar Naso Behaalotcha **Shelach** Korach Chukat Balak Pinchas Matot Masai

The Power of the Few

Friends, I agree with you in Providence; but I believe in the Providence of the most men, the largest purse, and the longest cannon. – Abraham Lincoln

Our individualistic society likes to give importance to the difference one person can make. We have innumerable accounts of how one person, standing up to many, overcomes public opinion, resistance, and ridicule and with faith and perseverance, triumphs against the odds of the many.

However, there is one area of human activity where most are of the opinion that numbers have a direct impact on results: War. Napoleon consistently overruns professional soldiers with masses of conscripted Frenchmen who marched over their well-ordered but fewer enemies. Though the Spartans held the Persians at the legendary Battle of Thermopylae for seven days, eventually superior Persian numbers won the day.

There are obvious exceptions. The battles of modern-day Israel have consistently pitted larger forces against smaller ones, with results that surprised the world. If we go back further in Jewish history we recall the victory of the humble Maccabeans against the mighty Syrio-Greco Empire in memory for which we still celebrate Chanukah more than two millennia later.

There is an unusual account in the Torah of a particularly unsuccessful Israelite battle. It occurs immediately after the Sin of the Spies, when the representatives of the Twelve Tribes returned from spying the land, gave a frightening report as to the strength of the Canaanite enemies and in turn caused panic and hysteria amongst the people of Israel. God punishes that generation of men to die in the desert and the entire Israelite nation to wander in the wilderness outside of Canaan for forty years.

However, after the punishment is decreed, men repent and issue a war cry, stating that they are not afraid and will proceed with the invasion of Canaan, as planned previously. But it is too late. Moses warns them that God is no longer with them and that they will fail. They ignore Moses' warning. They attack and are soundly defeated by the Canaanites.

The Baal Haturim on Numbers 14:40 states that we are talking about an Israelite army of 600,000 that was not able to defeat a much smaller enemy. However, he goes on to recall how biblical Jonathan (son of King Saul) with just the assistance of one lad was able to rout an entire Midianite army. God has no qualm to save with many or with few.

BERESHIT   SHEMOT   VAYIKRA   **BAMIDBAR**   DEVARIM   Baal Haturim
Bamidbar Naso Behaalotcha **Shelach** Korach Chukat Balak Pinchas Matot Masai

Dedication

To the upcoming wedding of Andrea Klotnicki and Bruno Zalcberg. May they always triumph against all odds.

Coward's Failure

"He who fears being conquered is sure of defeat." -Napoleon Bonaparte

Experience shows a direct correlation between courage and success on one hand and fear and failure on the other. That is not to say that fear is not normal or doesn't have its place, but it certainly worsens the odds of any victory.

Shortly before what was meant to be the historic and divinely-assisted conquest of the Promised Land, Moses sends twelve princes of Israel, a representative of each tribe, to spy out the land of Canaan. Ten weak-hearted amongst them see giants in the land and are terror-stricken.

When these spies return to Moses and the Jewish people to report the results of their mission, they make a curious remark: *"We were in our eyes as grasshoppers and so we were in their eyes."*

As poorly as they thought of themselves, that is how the fearful spies appeared in the eyes of their enemies. Their fear became their reality and redefined them, not only in their own perception, but in the perception of the world. The Netziv on Numbers 13:33 explains that with fear it is impossible to win. So while the spies' attitude was unfortunate and led to the punishment of forty years of wandering, in a sense they were correct that the young Jewish nation could not win. Their fear insured that there was no chance they would conquer the land in their time.

May we overcome our fears, take courage and experience victory.

Dedication

To the athletic warriors competing in the World Cup. Good luck!

BERESHIT SHEMOT VAYIKRA **BAMIDBAR** DEVARIM   Ibn Ezra
Bamidbar Naso Behaalotcha **Shelach** Korach Chukat Balak Pinchas Matot Masai

Jewish Anger Management

"Whoever is out of patience is out of possession of their soul." -Francis Bacon

In what seems like an almost incredible statement, Moses tells God to calm down. In the notorious story of the spies, the Children of Israel have upset God one time too many and He is ready to destroy them. Moses jumps into the fray and beseeches God to show "strength":

And now, I pray Thee, let the power of the Lord be great, as You have spoken, saying: The Lord is slow to anger, and plenteous in lovingkindness, forgiving iniquity and transgression, and that will by no means clear the guilty; visiting the iniquity of the fathers upon the children, upon the third and upon the fourth generation. Pardon, I pray Thee, the iniquity of this people according unto the greatness of Thy lovingkindness, and according as You have forgiven this people, from Egypt even until now.' And the Lord said: 'I have pardoned according to thy word.' Numbers 14:17-20

According to the sages and well-codified by Maimonides – anger is one of the worst traits possible and we must work hard to mitigate its expression.

Ibn Ezra explains how God was able to "overcome" His anger and what He needed to "strengthen". God, among His infinite, omnipotent, omnipresent, omniscient and other omni-traits is extremely patient (infinitely patient? Not sure about that one).

According to Ibn Ezra, God, because of the great level of patience that He possesses was able to "break" his anger by strengthening further, with Moses' cajoling, His patience. His anger was abated (somewhat) and instead of wiping out the people of Israel, He instead castigated the spies directly and doomed that generation to die slowly in the desert over the course of forty years of wandering, prohibited them from entering the promised land, leaving it instead for a less infuriating generation.

May we learn to strengthen our own levels of patience and break our anger whenever it rears its ugly head.

Dedication
To the complete and speedy recovery of Yosef Yehoshua ben Gila.

Detailed Devils, Vague Angels

"Some facts should be suppressed, or, at least, a just sense of proportion should be observed in treating them." -Sir Arthur Conan Doyle

Truth and factuality have been a prime tenet of Judaism so much so that Truth is considered God's "seal." The Torah has not shied away from revealing unflattering episodes of our ancestors. However, we have also seen some notable exceptions. There are some famous "bendings" of the truth, even by God Himself, in order to keep domestic peace.

What is less reported is not a bending of truth but a conscious omission of truth and facts. Early in the Israelite sojourn in the desert, Moses sends twelve spies to scout out the land. Their negative report is what then led to the punishment of forty years of desert wandering.

The Torah provides a fairly detailed description of the event, quoting what they said, where they went, what they did and the repercussions. Curiously, at one stage of the narrative, the Torah becomes suddenly vague and literally says "and they answered them **something**." (Hello! What did they answer them?").

The Ohr Hachayim (Numbers 13:26) explains that the Torah is being vague on purpose. The spies at this point are considered evil and what they did and said was bad. He states that the Torah does not wish to detail the deeds of the wicked unless it absolutely has to. He claims that unless there is a specific constructive purpose, the Torah will not disclose the indiscretions of others, even if they are deserving of public censure.

How much more so must we be careful in disclosing "facts" about others.

Dedication
To those who hold their tongue.

Korach

[Numbers Chapters XVI-XVIII]

BERESHIT SHEMOT VAYIKRA **BAMIDBAR** DEVARIM   Baal Haturim
Bamidbar Naso Behaalotcha Shelach **Korach** Chukat Balak Pinchas Matot Masai

Corruptibility
Remember, when the judgment's weak, the prejudice is strong. -K. O'Hara

The theme of justice runs strongly throughout the Torah. We are advised to pursue justice diligently. One of the first organizational efforts of the nascent nation of Israel is to create a justice system. Judges were appointed to represent every ten individuals, with a system of additional judges to handle cases that may have been too difficult for the parochial judges.

This court system is likewise warned of the danger of bribes, with the famous line that "the bribe will blind the sharp ones, and will corrupt the words of the wise."

The Baal Haturim on Numbers 18:19 explains that a judge's corruptibility is directly dependent on his financial situation. If the judge is independently wealthy "like a king," states the Baal Haturim, then his judgment and his rulings will be established and impervious to financial considerations. If, however, the judge is needy "like a Cohen," (the Cohen in biblical times was completely dependent on the donations, handouts and charity of the Israelite landowners), then his judgments and rulings will only lead to ruin, as he may have other pressures or considerations in mind, besides those of absolute justice.

May we reach levels of success that will make us incorruptible.

Dedication
To my teacher from many years ago, Rabbi Kalman Ber, current Chief Rabbi of the city of Netanya. It was an incredible surprise and delight to have him in Montevideo.

BERESHIT SHEMOT VAYIKRA **BAMIDBAR** DEVARIM   Netziv
Bamidbar Naso Behaalotcha Shelach **Korach** Chukat Balak Pinchas Matot Masai

Too Holy

"Fanatical religion driven to a certain point is almost as bad as none at all, but not quite." -Will Rogers

My Talmud instructor (Rebbe) at Yeshiva University (YU), Rabbi Shimon Romm of blessed memory, had a lasting impact on me. Since his childhood he was considered a Torah prodigy. He was an alumnus of the famed Mir Yeshiva that escaped the Nazis and ended up for a time in Shanghai. After Shanghai, he spent a number of years in Israel and subsequently moved to New York. At YU he was one of the only Rabbis that gave his classes in Hebrew. He had a photographic memory and a sharp sense of humor.

A line I heard from him often was "don't be too religious". He was particularly acerbic against the growing movement of Jews who continually sought greater levels of strictures in the name of religion. In that sense, he mirrored the thoughts of the Netziv on the episode of Korach and his supporters.

In this week's Torah reading, two hundred and fifty men of ostensibly high religious standing join Korach's desert rebellion against the leadership of Moses and Aaron. Korach and his supporters are killed by very clear divine intervention, with the two hundred and fifty men being burned by divine fire when they bring incense as part of their effort to reach an even higher level than what they were at.

The Netziv warns in Numbers 16:1 that an attempt to reach too high in ones holiness can actually lead a person to go against basic commandments that God does demand we perform. It becomes ironic that a person seeking to become holier ends up failing in basic principles. The Netziv claims that though the person may get some credit for good intentions, they are nonetheless punished by God for their wrong-headed, holier-than-thou, anti-Torah acts.

As something else that Rabbi Romm would say: "Be a *mentsch* (well-behaved man) before trying to be a *tzaddik* (a holy man)."

May we aim for high levels of holiness, without forgetting the more fundamental commandments that are the basis of good, proper human relationships.

Dedication

To the safe and speedy return of Eyal, Gilad and Naftali.
Mazal Tov to our Akiva on his graduation from high school.

BERESHIT SHEMOT VAYIKRA **BAMIDBAR** DEVARIM　　　　Ibn Ezra
Bamidbar Naso Behaalotcha Shelach **Korach** Chukat Balak Pinchas Matot Masai

Destiny's Name

"The real test of a man is not how well he plays the role he has invented for himself, but how well he plays the role that destiny assigned to him." - Jan Patocka

The age of prophecy has long passed us by, however, the sages claim that there still remains one small spark of prophecy in our lives. That is the moment we name our children. Somehow, in that instant, there is divine inspiration or accord. The child is meant to have the name given and it is much more than a tag to call the child by. It carries some import, some significance that somehow will color the rest of their lives.

In this week's Torah reading, we have one personality that Ibn Ezra (on Numbers 18:2) explains lived up to his name. It is Levi, the forerunner of the Levite tribe. The word Levi in Hebrew has the same root as the word "to lend". Ibn Ezra states that the Levites as a whole are basically "lent" by the rest of Israel to the Cohens, to the Temple, with the purpose of participating and assisting in the holy service.

Sometimes a person's traits can be identified with their name immediately. Sometimes it takes an entire life to understand the connection. And sometimes we only understand generations later the impact that a person had and the connection to that tiny spark of prophecy that is their name.

May we live up to our good names.

Dedication

To the family of the Good Name and to the sixth grade girls of the Integral school and their parents on the celebration of their Bat-Mitzvah!

BERESHIT SHEMOT VAYIKRA **BAMIDBAR** *DEVARIM* Ohr Hachayim
Bamidbar Naso Behaalotcha Shelach **Korach** *Chukat Balak Pinchas Matot Masai*

Souls in Motion

"Our souls are not hungry for fame, comfort, wealth or power. Those rewards create almost as many problems as they solve. Our souls are hungry for meaning, for the sense that we have figured out how to live so that our lives matter, so that the world will be at least a little bit different for our having passed through it." -Rabbi Harold Kushner

Souls, just as objects, can be distinguished by those in motion and those at rest.

When navigating the spiritual realm, it may be useful to know the pecking order of the various categories of spirits floating around.

The Ohr Hachayim (Number 16:22) provides exactly such guidance, as follows:

1. God enjoys the singing and praise of the ministering angels, who do his bidding.

2. Above the angels, are the innocent human souls of those yet to be born, untainted as yet by sin.

3. Above the unborn are spirits of the righteous who have already negotiated the challenges of human life and whose souls have returned to the heavenly abode.

4. However, the highest level of spirit, the one that God loves the most is none other than the still-living human soul. He loves the person who is struggling with the material world, who does not see God clearly, who has hints as to His presence, but who nonetheless strives to do His will, to grow closer to God. That spirit is considered to be at the highest spiritual levels, above the perfect angels (1), above the innocent unborn souls (2) and above even the souls of the departed righteous (3).

Hence, a living, breathing soul, a soul in motion, is the most precious within the hierarchy of spirit-states.

May our spirits move ever higher.

Dedication

To my nephew, Yoel Epstein, on the occasion of his Bar-Mitzvah. May he rise from strength to strength, his spirit soaring high.

חקת

Chukat

[Numbers Chapters XIX-XXI]

BERESHIT SHEMOT VAYIKRA **BAMIDBAR** DEVARIM   Baal Haturim
Bamidbar Naso Behaalotcha Shelach Korach **Chukat** *Balak Pinchas Matot Masai*

Beware the Fool

Against stupidity; God Himself is helpless. -Yiddish Proverb

Judaism puts great value on intelligence and learning. One of the highest appellations one can be given is that of "Talmid Chacham" – a wise scholar. Conversely, Jewish tradition is disparaging of the ignoramus, called since Mishnaic times an "am haaretz" – literally "people of the land", but meaning a boor.

As the study of Torah is the cornerstone of Jewish life and practice, those who decide to be ignorant, those who do not engage in the Torah, those who do not become familiar with its contents, put themselves in a substandard position in the hierarchy of Jewish achievement.

The Baal Haturim on Numbers 19:2 highlights this reality with a particular law. The people of Israel had an obligation to give a regular contribution of produce to their local Cohen called "Truma". The Truma had a certain sanctity and the Cohen had to consume it in a state of ritual purity. However, we are warned that we should not give this contribution, we should not give Truma to a Cohen who is an "am haaretz". If the Cohen is an ignoramus, if the Cohen could not be bothered to learn the laws of the Torah, then he is not deserving of these special contributions.

May we always improve our familiarity and connection to the Torah and merit a myriad of blessings.

Dedication

To a Cohen Talmid Chacham, Dr. Shmuel Katz, on the opening of his sixth free dental clinic in Israel. May blessings come quickly his way and may he merit having some joyous weddings in the very near future.

Gentle Strength

"Rudeness is the weak man's imitation of strength." -Eric Hoffer

"Rotund" was the simplest way to describe the smiling, mild mannered professor who lectured us regarding ancient Near East archeology. However, what belied that gentle exterior was a martial arts master who could pulverize bricks with a single blow. During one particularly disruptive class the professor warned in a deceptively mild tone, which I remember decades later: "Don't confuse niceness with weakness." The class immediately quieted down.

Ancient enemies of Israel did confuse politeness with feebleness. Moses and the Israelites asked permission of the nations in their path in the desert to pass peacefully through their territory on their way to the Promised Land. According to the Netziv on Numbers 21:1, these nations assumed that Israel was nicely asking for permission because they didn't have the strength to pass by force of arms. The nations saw such politeness as a sign of weakness and marched to war upon the presumably feeble Israel. What ensued was a massacre. Israel completely destroyed the entire armies and leadership of the two attacking kings of Sichon and Og and conquered their entire territory in a swift decisive victory that caused the entire region to tremble in fear of the approaching Israelites.

May our enemies learn to fear us and may we show strength to people who don't understand gentleness.

Dedication

To Israel's army and security forces. May God protect them during their search for our sons: Eyal, Gilad and Naftali.

BERESHIT SHEMOT VAYIKRA **BAMIDBAR** DEVARIM   Ibn Ezra
Bamidbar Naso Behaalotcha Shelach Korach **Chukat** Balak Pinchas Matot Masai

Talk is Cheap

"Speak out in acts; the time for words has passed, and only deeds will suffice." -John Greenleaf Whittier

The people of Israel are thirsty and restless. They complain and demand water. Moses is worried. God tells him to take his staff and talk to the rock. Moses strikes the rock. God punishes Moses by prohibiting him from entering the land of Israel. This is one of the more confusing episodes in the Bible.

Why did God punish Moses? There are as many answers as there are Bible commentaries. Ibn Ezra chimes in with his own theory. What does Moses do right before he strikes the rock? He gives a speech. It is a curt, sharp speech, biting and sarcastic in its tone. It is highly unusual for Moses, though not unwarranted, given the excessive complaints of the people. In Numbers 20:10 Moses asks:

"Hear now, ye rebels; are we to bring you forth water out of this rock?"

Moses doesn't wait for an answer. He hits the rock (twice) and water gushes forth.

Ibn Ezra (on Numbers 20:8) claims that the sin of Moses was his speech. He didn't need a preamble. He didn't need to announce his plans in what was a negative, derogatory comment. He just needed to act. He needed to follow God's instructions and provide the people of Israel with water.

It is true that they may have deserved a reprimand and that before performing yet another miracle, this may have seemed like an opportune time. But according to Ibn Ezra he should have acted first and spoken later.

May we always remember that talk is cheap and that actions always speak louder than words.

Dedication

In memory of Leon Lempert and Solomon Gerstenfeld. Men of action.

BERESHIT SHEMOT VAYIKRA **BAMIDBAR** DEVARIM Ohr Hachayim
Bamidbar Naso Behaalotcha Shelach Korach **Chukat** Balak Pinchas Matot Masai

When "Sorry" Ain't Enough

"Remorse is the punishment of crime; repentance, its expiation. The former appertains to a tormented conscience; the latter to a soul changed for the better." -Joseph Joubert

Moses indubitably had a good relationship with God, if not the best that a human can aspire to. Multiple times, God threatens to destroy the Children of Israel for their sins but then Moses intercedes. He prays to God, he argues with God, he beseeches God. God is then appeased, God is convinced, God forgives.

However, at some points, it's not enough. God does punish. He punishes the Children of Israel multiple times throughout their sojourn in the desert. In one case, however, both the punishment and the forgiveness are unusual.

During the fortieth year of their trek through the desert, the Israelites, not for the first time, complain: *"Why did you bring us out of Egypt to die in this desert. There's no food, no water and we had enough of this manna."* (Numbers 21:5)

God sends fiery serpents that bite and kill a multitude of Israel. The people realize they've done something wrong, admit their sin and then beg Moses to pray on their behalf. Moses acquiesces and prays. God however, is not impressed. He tells Moses to make a serpent of copper. Only then, if a victim of the deadly bites looks up at the copper serpent are they saved. Otherwise they die.

The Ohr Hachayim (on Numbers 21:7) explains that the apology by the Israelites was not heartfelt. They understood intellectually that they were wrong, but they had not truly repented. Saying sorry was not enough. Only by looking heavenward, only by realizing, internalizing and reaffirming their faith in God, could they be saved. As long as they looked downward, as long as they kept God out of their hearts and souls, they died.

Lip service was not enough. Only by demonstrating their faith in God did they truly repent and achieve forgiveness. May our own sights be ever upward.

Dedication

To my cousins, Rabbi Yair and Nitza Spitz, on their departure to Toronto to take up important roles in the community. Good luck!

בלק

Balak

[Numbers Chapters XXII-XXV]

BERESHIT SHEMOT VAYIKRA **BAMIDBAR** DEVARIM   Baal Haturim
Bamidbar Naso Behaalotcha Shelach Korach Chukat **Balak** Pinchas Matot Masai

Perilous Roads

Life is a journey that must be traveled no matter how bad the roads and accommodations. -Oliver Goldsmith

Although ubiquitous and constant and despite the marvels of modern technology at our disposal, travel remains one of the most fatal human activities, with more people dying from transportation accidents then any other non-medical cause. The advent of smartphones has likely increased the dangers we all face.

The Baal Haturim on Numbers 22:22 states that all roads are to be considered a source of danger. It does not matter how accustomed to the road we are or how many times we've traveled it.

There is an ancient Jewish Law, that when one sets upon the road to go any distance outside ones city, they must say the Wayfarer's Prayer. It is a short, simple, direct prayer, beseeching God to protect us from the dangers of the road and to insure we reach our destination safely. We are so concerned about the pitfalls of travel that there is another short blessing of thanks (Birkat Hagomel) which is required for sea and air journeys that must be stated in a Minyan (a quorum of ten men). This is the same blessing as for one who was freed from prison, traversed the desert or recuperated from a bedridden illness.

May we take all appropriate physical, mental and spiritual precautions as we travel from place to place.

Dedication

To David Taragan, who would so expertly takes me safely from place to place.

BERESHIT   SHEMOT   VAYIKRA   **BAMIDBAR**   DEVARIM   Netziv
Bamidbar Naso Behaalotcha Shelach Korach Chukat **Balak** Pinchas Matot Masai

Beware the Curse

"An orphan's curse would drag to hell, a spirit from on high; but oh! more horrible than that, is a curse in a dead man's eye!" -Samuel Taylor Coleridge

An enemy with a slightly greater understanding of God's relationship to the Jewish people rises up against us. Balak the King of Moab, fears the Israelite approach to his kingdom. Though Israel merely wants to pass by peacefully and God has ordered Moses not to fight the Moabites, Balak nonetheless hires a powerful man to help with his struggle against Israel.

Balak understands that physical force cannot prevail against the Jewish nation. Therefore, he hires the sorcerer Bilaam, who is reputed to have the power to effectively curse whom he wants. What follows is an ironic, comical and embarrassing tale of Bilaam attempting to curse Israel and in three successive attempts, with God's direct involvement – blessings come out of Bilaam's mouth to the great chagrin of Balak.

The Netziv on Numbers 22:11 explains that the plan of this diabolical duo was faulty in its spiritual understanding. The Netziv states that curses only work where there is sin. At that moment in the desert when Bilaam set out to curse Israel, he could not see or find any sin. His attempts to curse would prove ineffective because there was no negative spiritual act for it to take a hold off.

Dedication

To the memory of Eyal, Gilad and Naftali for whom we mourn deeply.

BERESHIT SHEMOT VAYIKRA **BAMIDBAR** DEVARIM   Ibn Ezra
Bamidbar Naso Behaalotcha Shelach Korach Chukat **Balak** Pinchas Matot Masai

Chink in our Armor

"We must watch over our modesty in the presence of those who cannot understand its grounds." -Jean Rostand

The evil sorcerer, Bilaam, teams up with the powerful King of Moab, Balak, to destroy the people of Israel. Bilaam attempts time and again to blast magical curses against the Israelite nation. However, God intervenes, and Bilaam, instead of cursing Israel, is forced by God to bless Israel.

After three failed attempts, Bilaam is cast away by an enraged King Balak. Israel seemed impervious to any attack. According to Ibn Ezra on Numbers 23:21, Balak does not give up. God's very blessings provide Balak with a clue as to Israel's fatal weakness.

One of the blessings mentions that God found "no fault" in Israel. Balak then reasoned (correctly), that if God were to find fault in Israel, they would be vulnerable to curses and destruction. The Rabbis comment that the women of Israel, (and as a result also the men), were modest and faithful in their amorous activities, which pleased God. With this insider information King Balak organizes the seduction of the Israelite men and sends a squad of Moabite and Midianite women to the Israelite camp. Balak knew that if the Israelite men would fall to the prohibited charms of the idol-worshipping women, then God's impenetrable protection of the Jewish people would stop.

In this sexual attack, Balak is wildly successful. The Israelite men indeed succumb to the temptation, and then without lifting a finger, Balak witnesses God's own assault upon the people of Israel with a fatal plague that kills 24,000 Israelites in short order.

Not only does God no longer provide defense, but He Himself punishes us for not living and behaving as we are supposed to.

We have a potent armor in God's protection. We should be careful not to lose it.

Dedication

To the modest, understanding and forgiving people I dealt with this week. May God's protection always be with you.

BERESHIT SHEMOT VAYIKRA **BAMIDBAR** DEVARIM   Ohr Hachayim
Bamidbar Naso Behaalotcha Shelach Korach Chukat **Balak** Pinchas Matot Masai

The Drive of Destiny
"Fate leads the willing, and drags along the reluctant." -Seneca

Bilaam son of Beor was a particularly nasty character. He was no friend of ancient Israelites and rabbinic commentaries depict him as a completely evil sorcerer who was eternally damned. Nonetheless, he reached the heights of prophecy and technically is said to have achieved the level of divination of Moses himself.

The Ohr Hachayim (on Numbers 24:3) wonders as to the makeup of Bilaam and what attributes enabled him to achieve his prophetic proficiency. He identifies three characteristics: birth, work and destiny.

Bilaam was born with an innate capability to pierce the material world. His physical and mental attributes were such that he could more easily appreciate and interact with the spiritual world. However, the gifts of birth are not sufficient to accomplish anything.

Bilaam was a hard worker. He was ambitious, highly ambitious. He applied himself and learned all the dark arts. He mastered what was known to man about the supernatural. He commanded demons and directed kings. His hard work made him great, but that was not enough to account for his singular prophetic achievement (which led to his obliteration, but that's another story).

Bilaam was destined to reach prophecy. God required a gentile to reach the prophetic stature of Moses. God wanted the nations of the world to have their own figure that could commune more directly with God. True, Bilaam twisted his powers for his own avarice and consciously shunned the word of God. But he had the capacity. He had the skills. He had the connection. He was meant to reach prophecy, and that fate is what, together with his personal attributes and his work ethic drew him to the pinnacle of the spiritual world (for a brief moment, anyway).

May we follow a fortunate fate and desist from dreary destiny.

Dedication
To Julie Grey, a Hollywood master wordsmith and fellow blogger. Welcome to Israel. To intertwined fates and glorious destiny.

פנחס

Pinchas

[Numbers Chapters XXV-XXIX]

BERESHIT SHEMOT VAYIKRA **BAMIDBAR** DEVARIM Baal Haturim
Bamidbar Naso Behaalotcha Shelach Korach Chukat Balak **Pinchas** Matot Masai

Secrets of Creation

This most beautiful system The Universe could only proceed from the dominion of an intelligent and powerful Being. -Sir Isaac Newton

The Talmud warns us not to delve too deeply into the origins of the Universe. It further states that those who are privy to the secrets of creation should only transmit them to worthy students, and even then only in private discussions.

As Moses prepares to pass the reigns of leadership to his disciple Joshua, the Baal Haturim on Numbers 27:20 reveals that Moses also transmitted to Joshua the secrets of the "Merkava" and of creation.

The "Merkava" (literally, Chariot) refers to the prophetic visions documented by Ezekiel as to the divine presence. It is a very deep, esoteric study which preoccupies many kabbalists. Creation is likewise veiled by the mists of time. Even with various scientific theories and advances, we cannot easily answer some of the most basic questions as to how or why we have the particular physical universe we're familiar with.

However, it was important for at least the spiritual leaders of the generation to have some familiarity with these fundamental concepts, to know, from tradition, what the elemental forces and functioning of both our spiritual and physical existence are.

Dedication

To Paco Diez, composer, singer and leading disseminator of traditional Sepharadic music. His concert in Montevideo was a spiritual experience.

Purposeful Reward

"Each of our acts makes a statement as to our purpose." -Leo Buscaglia

It is one of the more violently graphic scenes in the Torah. Pinchas, grandson of Aaron the High Priest, takes a spear and in one blow kills a prince of Israel as well as a Moabite princess as they are being publicly intimate. The scene of this gruesome double murder is in front of the otherwise unresponsive leadership of Israel.

This fierce act is credited with stopping a sudden plague that killed 24,000 people in Israel for the sin of illicit relations. In what is perhaps the most surprising and ironic outcome of Pinchas' vigilantism is that God bestows Pinchas with a "Covenant of Peace" and includes him in the prestigious caste of the Priesthood (to be a Kohen).

The Netziv on Numbers 25:13 explains that Pinchas' reward is a natural outcome of his act. What Pinchas was in essence doing when he killed the overly affectionate lovers was *protecting* the Jewish people from a virulent licentiousness that had reached so far and with such fervor that a prince of Israel was ready to perform such an act publicly in front of the leaders of the nation. Pinchas stops the decadence dead in its tracks (literally).

For taking such a principled stand and for being ready to protect the nation of Israel from such immorality Pinchas is rewarded with the charge of continuing to protect the Jewish people. That was the classical task of the Kohen; to educate the nation of Israel as to God's laws and traditions, to serve as role models of service of God and to thereby protect the Jewish people from the danger and damage of immorality.

May we each have the good fortune of finding our purposes and the reward of being able to fulfill that purpose.

Dedication

To the many and varied protectors of Israel and to our son Eitan who joined their forces this week.

BERESHIT SHEMOT VAYIKRA **BAMIDBAR** DEVARIM   Ibn Ezra
Bamidbar Naso Behaalotcha Shelach Korach Chukat Balak **Pinchas** Matot Masai

The Power of Honoring

"Example is the school of mankind, and they will learn at no other" - Edmund Burke

God has informed Moses of his impending forced retirement. Moses will not cross the Jordan River with the people of Israel to enter the promised land. Rather, God tells him that he will ascend the mountain, see the land, and die there outside of Canaan. Moses makes a final request of God: don't leave the people leaderless – appoint someone to follow me.

God acquiesces to the request and informs Moses that his disciple Joshua will take over the reins of leadership. Joshua is the one that will lead the people into Canaan and conquer the land.

In the first act of "semicha" or ordination, Moses places his hands upon Joshua and transmits to him some of his spirit, his glory, his authority. Ibn Ezra on Numbers 27:20 is so impressed by this act that he claims it had the immediate effect of raising Joshua's status in the eyes of the entire nation. By Moses honoring Joshua so, by raising Joshua to his own level, he showed the highest form of respect. The people of Israel immediately understood the action of Moses, the honor that he was showing Joshua, and they learned to honor Joshua as well, following Moses' example.

May we always have opportunity to see deserving people honored.

Dedication

To the chain of tradition, that has continued from Moses until this day. See here for an interesting presentation showing the unbroken chain of ordination that includes some of my Rabbis.

Personal, Pure, Public

Pinhas the Priest grabs a spear and personally skewers an amorous Israelite prince and his prohibited heathen paramour in a public display of zealotry that has been recorded for eternity (Numbers Chapter 25). God is then effusive with his compliments and gratitude and eternally rewards Pinhas for his extreme actions. Pinhas has since been lauded by Rabbinic commentators throughout the generations as the paradigm of successful (and hard to emulate) zealotry.

The Ohr Hachayim (on Numbers 25:11) attempts to understand the secret of Pinhas' wild success. He attributes three factors:

1. **Personally.** Pinhas committed his zealotry personally. He didn't delegate it to somebody else. He didn't outsource. He didn't command some underling to undertake the dangerous assignment. He did it himself with his own two hands, despite the very real personal danger (commentators explain that if any one aspect of Pinhas' attack would have gone wrong, Pinhas himself would have been killed).

2. **Purely.** Pinhas' intentions were pure. He had no ulterior motive. He had nothing personal against his adversaries. They were desecrating God's name and Pinhas' goal was solely to correct that grave infraction.

3. **Publicly.** Pinhas was not ashamed of his actions. He killed the prince in front of the entire nation. He believed so much in his cause, he had nothing to hide. It was done openly without any attempt to cover up any aspect.

So in short, the Ohr Hachayim's lesson for wild success is simply not to be afraid. Not to be afraid to do things personally; not to be afraid to do things with pure motivation; and not to be afraid to do things publicly. To do the right thing personally, to do it purely and to do it publicly is an unbeatable combination.

Dedication

To distant cousin and swimming zealot, Mark Spitz. He can teach a thing or two about wild success.

מטות

Matot

[Numbers Chapters XXX-XXXII]

*BERESHIT   SHEMOT   VAYIKRA   **BAMIDBAR**   DEVARIM*   Baal Haturim
Bamidbar Naso Behaalotcha Shelach Korach Chukat Balak Pinchas **Matot** *Masai*

A Leader's Vow
Vows are made in storms and forgotten in calm weather. -Thomas Fuller

One of the more disturbing stories in the Bible is that of the Israelite leader, Yiftah, in the Book of Judges. He was an outcast, but apparently with some leadership qualities. He attracted and led a band of ruffians. When the people of Israel are threatened, the elders turn to Yiftah for military assistance.

Before battle Yiftah takes an oath, that if God gives him victory over his enemies, in thanksgiving, Yiftah will sacrifice to God the first thing to greet him upon his successful return home. Perhaps Yiftah imagined a lamb would run to him, or some other livestock would cross his path. However, upon Yiftah's successful victory and subsequent return, none other than his beloved daughter, his only child, runs out to greet her victorious father. Yiftah tears his clothing in anguish, and the simplest reading of the verses indicate that he does kill his daughter as a human sacrifice to God.

The Baal Haturim on Numbers 30:2 explains that it is the nature of Israelite leaders to make vows and call for divine intervention when their people are in trouble. However, all the Rabbis are in agreement that Yiftah erred grievously, first, in making such a poorly worded vow, and second, in fulfilling such a dastardly act that is abhorrent to God. There is a procedure in Jewish law for rescinding poorly made vows that Yiftah should have availed himself of.

May we avoid vows. But if we make them, we should make them wisely and fulfill them honorably.

Dedication
To Miriam Cohen of Melbourne. May any and all vows be filled with blessings.

BERESHIT SHEMOT VAYIKRA **BAMIDBAR** DEVARIM   Netziv
Bamidbar Naso Behaalotcha Shelach Korach Chukat Balak Pinchas Matot Masai

After the Foxhole

"Vows are made in storms and forgotten in calm weather." -Thomas Fuller

We understand the concept of there being no atheists in a foxhole, of the rediscovery of God in the midst of danger. However, what is curious is our attitudes once the threat or need has passed. There is an example of a man late for an important meeting, urgently seeking a parking spot. He prays to God: "God, please help me find a spot and I promise I'll give a thousand dollars to charity." He keeps looking and prays even more fervently. "God! Help me with a spot and I'll give two thousand dollars to charity!" Suddenly, a spot opens up. The man parks and then calls out to God: "God, don't worry about it. I found a spot on my own!"

The instinctive search for God in times of distress seems to be counterbalanced by the just as natural tendency to forget about God once things are on an even keel. The Netziv on 30:2 warns about this phenomena when the Torah discusses the theme of vows. He explains that it is normal to make vows when distressed and just as normal for those earnest, heartfelt vows to slip our minds just moments later.

But God remembers the vow. According to Jewish law, the promises we make are binding. It has the weight and strength of a contract. We are morally obliged to fulfill our word even if it was uttered in a time of crisis. We must beware of oath-breaking.

May we feel free to call out to God in need, be careful with what we say, and have the perception, memory and will to deliver on our promises.

Dedication

To the victims of the AMIA terrorist bombing in Buenos Aires, twenty years ago, this week. And to the continued safety and protection of all those under threat in Israel.

Jealous and Vengeful God

"I had rather be a toad, and live upon the vapor of a dungeon than keep a corner in the thing I love for others uses."-William Shakespeare

There is a dark and dangerous side to our God and beware all who may unleash it. We believe in His mercy, but also in His justice. There is a divine fairness in His eternal plans that no human will ever fathom. However, we also witness His wrath, His anger, the death and destruction he lets loose upon the earth.

In the Bible we see two general victims of His wrath. Perhaps ironically, He is most angry at the people of Israel. Every infraction, every betrayal of the ancient covenant brings hardship, poverty, famine, conquerors, exile, persecution and even death. But there is also the element of mercy. He punishes Israel but does not obliterate Israel. The second types of victim of God's castigation are those who hurt Israel. There God has shown less restraint.

During our desert wanderings, the Midianite nation had participated in the enticement of the men of Israel. Israel turned to the worship of other gods, and God was swift with his response, the death by plague of 24,000 of Israel. But for the Midianites, God almost wipes them off the map. Every single male Midianite was killed and almost all of the females as well. Ibn Ezra on Numbers 31:3 explains that God commanded vengeance upon both His honor as well as Israel's. God saw it as one and the same. Like a jealous husband, God takes deep affront at both the seduction and injury of his people. If we think of all the empires, regimes and peoples that sought to harm the nation of Israel and wonder how many are still around, history will provide a very short list.

May the list get shorter.

Dedication
To hateful regimes of the world. You will be just a memory.

BERESHIT SHEMOT VAYIKRA **BAMIDBAR** DEVARIM   Ohr Hachayim
Bamidbar Naso Behaalotcha Shelach Korach Chukat Balak Pinchas **Matot** Masai

Individuality in the Crowd

I have a visceral aversion to crowds. I'm not sure where it stems from. Perhaps the days of getting trampled at protests, with only bruised toes and ribs to show for my idealism. Perhaps it's the anonymity in the horde. Or perhaps the mindless force of a mob.

There was a short sci-fi story I read once (if anyone remembers the title, *please* let me know) that depicted people waiting on line, or crowds, or any other assembly of humans that suddenly could not disperse. They became glued to each other – a multi-legged, multi-headed monster that moved around wildly and aimlessly, gobbling up the few independent humans remaining.

Western philosophy has taught us to eschew crowds and conformity, to laud individuality and difference. Nonetheless, the power of the crowd is inescapable. There is strength in numbers, might in a mob. But one might ask, what is the value of just one more person to an assembly, does one more voice, does one more individual really make a difference in a crowd?

The Ohr Hachayim (on Numbers 32:20) seems to think so. When Moses discusses the upcoming conquest of Canaan with the two (and a half) tribes that were to settle the eastern side of the Jordan River, he implies a distinct advantage in having these otherwise extraneous tribes join the invasion. Victory had been assured by God Himself. Why not let the tribesmen remain with their families as opposed to inflicting them with the fourteen-year separation that ensued?

The Ohr Hachayim answers: **"one cannot compare the merit of 100 people to the merit of 101 people."** There is an order of magnitude difference between 100 people and 101 people. To us it may seem like merely another digit has been added to our count, but in other ways, in ways that we can only imagine, the difference of one person, even amongst many others, makes a world of a difference.

May we always be counted with others for good things.

Dedication

To the memory of Rabbi Elyashiv and the close to 300,000 individuals that attended his funeral.

To the victims of the Burgas terror attack.

מסעי

Masai

[Numbers Chapters XXXIII-XXXVII]

BERESHIT SHEMOT VAYIKRA **BAMIDBAR** DEVARIM   Netziv
Bamidbar Naso Behaalotcha Shelach Korach Chukat Balak Pinchas Matot *Masai*

It's not the journey, it's the purpose

"There are many paths to the top of the mountain, but only one view." - Harry Millner

In my mad rush to book a last minute flight to Israel, I had to study multiple itineraries, websites, schedules and jump through too many web hoops. Flights that I finally managed to reserve suddenly changed prices and eventually disappeared altogether. Reservations that were made were then canceled by the airline. Finally, I got a flight which, as of this writing, I hope will still see me through on my journey to the Holy Land.

Netziv on Numbers 33:1 notes that the term "their journeys" is repeated three times at the introduction of the summary of the stops which Israel made since leaving Egypt until they were about to enter Canaan. He explains that each repetition represents a different purpose for the journey, that the purpose defines the journey and each journey or path requires a separate introduction.

The first leg of the Israelite journey was the Exodus from Egypt with a stopover at Mount Sinai to receive the divine revelation of the Torah, with the final purpose of entering the land of Canaan. However, the mission of the spies went awry and doomed the tribes of Israel to wander in the desert for forty years. The wandering was the second leg of their journey. The third and final leg of the journey was the resumption of the initial purpose – to enter the land of Israel.

Sometimes the journey is defined by its purpose, and to fulfill it, you have to reach the destination. The journey itself becomes secondary.

Dedication
To Dani Baruch of Adventour, for helping me with my journey.

דברים

Devarim

[Deuteronomy Chapters I-III]

Sufficient Scholars?

Excess generally causes reaction, and produces a change in the opposite direction, whether it be in the seasons, or in individuals, or in governments. -Plato

There is a belief in Jewish tradition, that the merits of a Torah scholar, of a "Talmid Chacham", that dedicates himself exclusively to studying Torah the entire day, provides a physical protection to the Jewish population around him. The mere act of profoundly and deeply reading and reviewing the ancient texts, of immersing oneself in the sea of Torah scholarship affords to others a divine safeguard against the evils of the world.

While this is an old, long-held belief, in recent decades it has become a more popular and underlying philosophy for growing segments of the Jewish nation. One question that may be asked is what is the ideal required ratio of these "spiritual defenders" as compared to the population being protected. How many of our sons should dedicate themselves to what otherwise might be considered activities that don't contribute materially to society? How many Torah scholars do we require as compared to active soldiers? How many people should be working for a living and how many should confine themselves to the four walls of the study hall as a career path?

Interestingly enough, the Baal Haturim provides an answer. He states on his commentary to Deuteronomy 1:3 that one "Talmid Chacham", one true Torah scholar, has the capacity to "protect" 40,000 people. For every 40,000 residents, one Talmid Chacham is enough. So for example, for a population of 8,000,000, the math would indicate that we would want 200 full-time professional Torah scholars.

One would therefore hope that the quality, commitment and seriousness of thousands upon thousands of men who ostensibly dedicate their lives exclusively to Torah study will afford us great protection.

Dedication
To the true Torah scholars out there.

BERESHIT   SHEMOT   VAYIKRA   BAMIDBAR   **DEVARIM**   Ibn Ezra
Devarim Vaetchanan Ekev Reeh Shoftim Ki Tetze Ki Tavo Nitzavim Vayelech Haazinu Vezot Habracha

Striking While Hot

"There is no avoiding war; it can only be postponed to the advantage of others." -Niccolo Machiavelli

Millennia ago, perhaps the first technological profession, blacksmithing, taught us to strike iron while it's hot. If you wait too long, if you wait until the red-hot metal has cooled down, your blows will be ineffective, your effort wasted, your resources spent, your time lost.

On the retelling of the journey of the tribes of Israel from Egypt towards Canaan, there is a curious statement which claims that the Jewish nation was only eleven days away from their destination, if they crossed into Canaan from the south. For a journey that eventually took forty years, it is an unusually short amount of time, making the decades-long trek particularly tragic, especially to an entire generation of soldiers that died in the desert and never merited to see the Promised Land. Furthermore, the direction the Israelite people finally entered Canaan was from the eastern border and not the southern one. So why does the Torah include this ironic and geographically misleading reminder of our wasted opportunity?

The Netziv on Deuteronmy 1:2 explains that at the time of the Exodus, the nations of the world were terrified of Israel. They had all heard of the ten plagues, the parting of the sea and the miraculous and complete destruction of the armed forces of the Egyptian Empire, the mightiest nation on the planet. The countries on the border of Canaan, specifically the nation of Seir on the southern border, would have scattered out of the way to let the Children of Israel cross through their territory. However, forty years later, Israel was no longer feared. Seir stood fearlessly in the path of Israel. Israel had to take the long road. They needed to march all the way around, eastward and northward and then to head back west towards the Jordan River and only then start their long withheld conquest of the land.

May our leadership and our soldiers strike well, strike hard, strike fast, and may all enemies of our people be destroyed quickly and thoroughly.

Dedication

To Captain Roni Kaplan for his own work against the media terrorists, to all our troops and to the entire family of Israel that supports them.

BERESHIT SHEMOT VAYIKRA BAMIDBAR **DEVARIM** Ibn Ezra

Devarim Vaetchanan Ekev Reeh Shoftim Ki Tetze Ki Tavo Nitzavim Vayelech Haazinu Vezot Habracha

Home Protection

"Home is a name, a word, it is a strong one; stronger than magician ever spoke, or spirit ever answered to, in the strongest conjuration." -Charles Dickens

Most people have a visceral connection, not necessarily to the physical construct, but rather to the emotional reality that they call home. It may be good, it may be bad, (it is rarely indifferent), but it is clearly emotional.

And whenever that home is threatened, in whatever form, the reaction is often instinctive, unthinking, responding from our guts and hearts.

The Bible recounts how after the sin of the spies and the punishment of wandering, a feisty group of men arose that defied the edict and ventured to conquer Canaan. Moses uses unusually flowery language in describing the result of the ill-planned attack: *"And they chased you like bees."* – Deuteronomy 1:44

Ibn Ezra explains that the moment someone attempts to harm a bee's home they will immediately attack and sting the aggressor. They have a natural, healthy, correct response to a threat to their family's dwelling.

May our homes ever remain safe from all harm and threats.

Dedication

To those expelled from Gush Katif on the eighth anniversary of that crime. May they continue to rebuild their homes and lives.

BERESHIT SHEMOT VAYIKRA BAMIDBAR **DEVARIM**   *Ohr Hachayim*
Devarim *Vaetchan at Ekev Reeh Shoftim Ki Tetze Ki Tavo Nitzavim Vayelech Haazinu Vezot Habracha*

Just Call My Name...
"... and I'll be there." - *James Taylor*

Knowing the True Name of someone is believed to confer some power by the user of the name upon the entity being named. In some cultures, a person's true or secret name is a closely guarded treasure that is only shared with ones most intimate circle. The True Name of God was likewise rarely disclosed even during Temple times, and today we have no public knowledge of it. However, in Judaism, God has many names and appellations that we still use to this day and which still may retain some power.

One of the Ten Commandments (the third one, to be precise) is not to take God's name in vain. God doesn't want us to use His name lightly. There is a matter of respect, of distance, of awe that must be maintained. But God also wants to have a relationship with us. He is a loving, caring, involved God and He wants us to talk to Him, to pray to Him, to call on Him - but that's hard to do if you don't use His name. (note: curious that the vernacular term for God in Hebrew is "The Name") The solution is of course, to use His name properly. To use it in prayer. To use it in giving Him thanks. To use it in celebration and in mourning. However, there is one unusual circumstance where we can also use His name: in combating evil. (Can't you see it now, some superhero, in his cape and tights, yelling: "By God, you villain! I will strike you down in the name of the Almighty!")

The Ohr Hachayim (on Deuteronomy 1:10) quotes the Kabalistic tome, the Zohar (3:112) and states that whenever God's name is mentioned (properly) no evil can befall. Wow! (see this week's fiction chapter below for dramatic use of this idea).

May we learn to use God's name correctly and be spared from all evil.

Dedication
To the memory of Maurice Shashoua.

ואתחנן

Vaetchanan

[Deuteronomy Chapters III-VIII]

BERESHIT SHEMOT VAYIKRA BAMIDBAR **DEVARIM** Baal Haturim
Devarim **Vaetchanan** Ekev Reeh Shoftim Ki Tetze Ki Tavo Nitzavim Vayelech Haazinu Vezot Habracha

Anti-Demon Laser
Only when your consciousness is totally focused on the moment you are in, can you receive whatever gift, lesson, or delight that moment has to offer. -Barbara De Angelis

We are all chased by demons at some point in our lives. Either real ones, or metaphorical ones. They may gnaw at your consciousness. They may invade your dreams. They may dominate your nightmares. However, when they intrude upon your daily life, it becomes a dangerous threat.

The Baal Haturim on Deuteronomy 6:4 provides a prescription for the banishment of demons. It is the age-old prayer of "Shma Israel". It is the prayer that our Patriarch Jacob is said to have recited upon his emotional reunion with his long-lost son, Joseph. It is the prayer that countless Jewish martyrs throughout the ages stated with their dying breath as they were hung, flayed, burned, shot and gassed to death. It is the rallying call of the Jewish faithful to our one God.

The Baal Haturim explains that when a person recites the prayer of "Shma Israel" with earnest concentration, not only does it ward off and protect a person from demons; it actually causes demons to flee from that person.

May we choose to focus and concentrate on the important and meaningful moments in our day.

Dedication
To the Zlatkin family on their return to Israel. Godspeed.

Seeing is Doing

"To perceive means to immobilize... we seize, in the act of perception, something which outruns perception itself." -Henri Bergson

The Observer Effect is a physical phenomenon that posits that the act of observation affects in some fashion whatever is being observed. This has been confused with the related Heisenberg Uncertainty Principle, which makes different but related claims.

At the end of his life, Moses begs God to allow him to enter the Promised Land and retract the punishment prohibiting him from entering Canaan. God remains adamant, but as some type of consolation grants Moses the privilege of seeing the land of Israel.

The Netziv on 3:27 claims that God granted Moses the ability to "sense" the land with more than just his eyes. That somehow his vision enhanced his other senses and that Moses perceived the land in some fashion as if he were walking on it. Furthermore, Moses' viewing of the land was so powerful and had such an effect, that it actually ensured that Joshua's conquest of the land would be successful.

May all those who come to view the land of Israel and walk on it, may all those who come to support its soldiers, merit to see the success, security and safety of all our people.

Dedication

To the bereaved families of the fallen soldiers. To the mothers, fathers, wives, fiancées, brothers, sisters, sons and daughters. We are with you in your mourning.

BERESHIT SHEMOT VAYIKRA BAMIDBAR **DEVARIM**　　　　*Ibn Ezra*
Devarim **Vaetchanan** Ekev Reeh Shoftim Ki Tetze Ki Tavo Nitzavim Vayelech Haazinu Vezot Habracha

Give me Addiction or Give me Death

"Within yourself deliverance must be searched for, because each man makes his own prison."-Sir Edwin Arnold

It is easy to fall into a pattern. It is easy to find something enjoyable or convenient in your life and stick to it. At first we like it. Later we seek it. At more advanced stages we may rely on it and at the end we can't live without it. That most advanced stage has many names. A modern term is addiction. An ancient term is enslavement.

The book of Deuteronomy goes to the trouble of repeating the Ten Commandments that were given at Mount Sinai forty years earlier and recorded in the book of Exodus. There are some interesting differences between the two versions, but one of them is the recounting of the fourth commandment to Keep Holy the Sabbath.

The first mention of the commandment in Exodus is more universalistic, connecting the observance of the Sabbath to the Creation story. The second mention in Deuteronomy is more particular to the Jewish experience of the Egyptian enslavement and eventual exodus.

Ibn Ezra on Deuteronomy 5:14 explains that we must remember the Sabbath *because* we were slaves. We must take at least one day a week to release ourselves from the bonds of servitude. The real question to ask is what are we slaves to today and how do we break free?

Dedication

To our son, Netanel, on the occasion of his putting on his tefillin for the first time.

Too much prayer?

*"Longevity, Children and Livelihood are not dependant on Merit, but rather on **Mazal** (luck)."* – Rava, Babylonian Talmud, Moed Katan 28a.

There is a commonly held belief in Judaism, propagated most popularly in recent generations by followers of some Hassidic groups, that wherever there is some lack or deficiency in human aspirations, it is due to a lack of prayer or righteousness. While this may be true for many people and in many cases, when this principle is taken to an extreme, it is not only wrong – it is dangerous.

Was Moses not righteous enough or did not pray enough for his wish to cross into Israel? Do parents not pray enough for the health of their sick or dying children? Are innocent children lacking in righteousness when they are stricken down? No. It is a fallacy to think that lack of prayer or righteousness is at fault for every situation.

The Ohr Hachayim (on Deuteronomy 6:5) brings the above referenced quote to make a point that may frustrate (or end the frustration engendered by) the belief that prayer or righteousness is the answer to all our needs. Observant Jews read the "Shmah" twice daily as a prime article of faith. The second verse states:

"And you shall love God, your Lord, with all of your heart, with all of your soul, and with all of your means."

The Ohr Hachayim explains that **heart** equals **children**, **soul** equals **longevity**, and **means** equals **livelihood**. Not everyone is blessed with children, longevity or livelihood. Some who are blessed with these gifts may see it suddenly torn away from them. According to the Ohr Hachayim it does not demonstrate a lack of prayer or righteousness.

He adds that the objective of our statement of faith, is that even if God were to hold back or take these things from us, despite ones physical and spiritual efforts, we need to retain our faith in Him; in His justice, mercy and loving-kindness. We do not know what *Mazal* we are born under. We do not know the divine calculations. We can pray. We can do good deeds. But we cannot judge. We cannot believe on one hand that God is unjust or on the other hand that a person has failed in his righteousness or his efforts. We just can't understand, and those who claim they do – well, I'd steer clear of them.

May we have the Mazal of healthy children, robust longevity and ample livelihood.

BERESHIT SHEMOT VAYIKRA BAMIDBAR **DEVARIM**   Ohr Hachayim
Devarim Vaetchanan Ekev Reeh Shoftim Ki Tetze Ki Tavo Nitzavim Vayelech Haazinu Vezot Habracha

Dedication

To all those blessed to have completed the seven and a half year cycle of study of the Bablyonian Talmud and especially to my wife and the other dedicated women of Alon Shvut. You are inspirational.

עקב

Ekev

[Deuteronomy Chapters VIII-XI]

BERESHIT SHEMOT VAYIKRA BAMIDBAR **DEVARIM** Baal Haturim
Devarim Vaetchanan **Ekev** Reeh Shoftim Ki Tetze Ki Tavo Nitzavim Vayelech Haazinu Vezot Habracha

Fashionable Resurrections

If that vital spark that we find in a grain of wheat can pass unchanged through countless deaths and resurrections, will the spirit of man be unable to pass from this body to another? -William Jennings Bryan

It is a principle of Jewish faith that at some point in the future, the dead will come back to life. We have it listed as 13th of Maimonides 13 Principles of Faith: **"I believe with complete faith that there will be a revival of the dead when it will rise up the will from the Creator, blessed be His Name."**

This precept raises multiple questions:
- In what body will we return?
- Will we return old or young?
- If we suffered the loss of a limb, will we return whole?
- If you believe in reincarnation, which person will return?
- And finally, will we return dressed or naked?

While I have faith that all of these questions will be taken care of satisfactorily, the Baal Haturim does provide in Deuteronomy 8:3 the answer to at least one of the questions. He states that the resurrected will return fully clothed. He gives the analogy to wheat. If a seed of wheat can be buried in the ground "naked", decompose, and return fully grown and "clothed" then so too, those destined to return from death will return fully clothed.

One less thing to worry about.

Dedication
To all innocent victims of violence.

BERESHIT SHEMOT VAYIKRA BAMIDBAR **DEVARIM** Netziv
Devarim Vaetchanan **Ekev** Reeh Shoftim Ki Tetze Ki Tavo Nitzavim Vayelech Haazinu Vezot Habracha

Unusual Success

"The supernatural is the natural not yet understood." -Elbert Hubbard

As modern men of science, we are in love with the laws of cause and effect. This is true not only in the physical laws, but also in the social and economic laws. This linear thinking certainly dominates the world of business, where one expects that thorough research, good planning, intelligent decisions, skilled personnel and hard work should ostensibly lead to success.

While all these things are generally prerequisites, we are still witnesses to abysmal failures of well executed and well funded ventures as well as the uncommon successes of businesses that one can only say that extreme "luck" was on their side.

The Netziv on Deuteronomy 7:13 introduces another unusual source of success. According to the Netziv the study of Torah, the daily encounter and familiarization with Jewish law and tradition is an uncommon source of blessings. He states that by learning Torah, God bestows blessings over and above the laws of nature. There is some supernatural power in the study of the Torah that can have an influence beyond the rational.

Let's take advantage and reach for those supernatural blessings.

Dedication

To Robin Williams. You were an uncommon success who made us laugh. We will miss you.

For a speedy recovery of Jackeline Denise Eliana bat Ana Osnat.

BERESHIT SHEMOT VAYIKRA BAMIDBAR **DEVARIM**   *Ibn Ezra*
Devarim Vaetchanan **Ekev** *Reeh Shoftim Ki Tetze Ki Tavo Nitzavim Vayelech Haazinu Vezot Habracha*

The Illusion of Reality
"Reality is nothing but a collective hunch." -Lily Tomlin

One of the more insightful films of recent years was the popular "The Matrix" produced by the Wachowski Brothers. The writers imagined a reality that was a sophisticated illusion. Humanity it turned out was dormant, dreaming a collective dream as the machines fed upon human energy. However, the dream felt real. All of the senses were engaged. The brains of the trapped humans saw, felt, heard, smelled and tasted what they perceived as reality.

Only a select minority was free of The Matrix and saw reality for what it was. Ibn Ezra on Deuteronomy 8:3 alludes that our world may also be merely a façade for a deeper reality. He explains that the Children of Israel did not live on bread, but rather by the more divinely obvious Ma'an that descended from the heavens daily. He correlates the bread to the courser, more material, physical reality, while the Ma'an is much more representative of the deeper reality of God's underlying power and will, which is what truly sustains our existence.

May we see through the illusions of our life to the profound truths of our universe.

Dedication
To the people on different sides of the planet who assisted us in many timely and stress-relieving ways in the reality of moving from one existence to an apparently different one. Though the strain may be a temporal illusion, the relief and friendship are real.

BERESHIT SHEMOT VAYIKRA BAMIDBAR **DEVARIM** Ohr Hachayim
Devarim Vaetchanan **Ekev** Rech Shoftim Ki Tetze Ki Tavo Nitzavim Vayelech Haazinu Vezot Habracha

Imperialistic Israel

"I will insist that the Hebrews have done more to civilize men than any other nation ... fate had ordained the Jews to be the most essential instrument for civilizing the nations." -John Adams (1735-1826)

Europe is an economic mess, the height of the American empire seems to be in the past, and the question of China as the next superpower still remains a question. Israel on the other hand is proving itself to be economically strong and one of the leading exporters of vital technology to the world.

The Jewish nation has continuously astounded the world, both throughout its long Diaspora and more recently since the founding of the State of Israel. Since the destruction of the second Temple two thousand years ago Jews have found themselves at the centers of power and at the forefront of revolution, discovery and imagination. What makes the Jew insinuate himself into the vanguard of society and where is this constructive infiltration leading?

The Ohr Hachayim (on Deuteronomy 7:12) indicates that it is a matter of fate. He claims that in some promised future, the Jewish people are destined to dominate the entire world. I don't believe it will be in the villainous and fabricated scenario portrayed in the 'Protocols of the Elders of Zion' and not even in the geographic, financial or military might of previous empires, but rather in a more positive and subtle way, one that the Hebrew nation has been preparing for millennia.

The Jewish empire that has been developing throughout most of history is one of influence, culture, ethics, values and meaning. You see the Jew with an outsized proportion of impact in almost every arena of human activity. With a state of its own, this impact has become a major export business with a clearly defined center and incubator. Much has been written on the subject and much more will be written (and I hope to contribute further on this, so stay tuned for more).

In my opinion, Israel is the next superpower – and I'm glad to be part of it.

Dedication

To all the people and organizations cheerleading Israel (their numbers seem to be growing). We're on the right track. Anyone with supporting factoids, vignettes and articles, please send them to me for an upcoming book on how Israel is becoming the next superpower.

ראה

Reeh

[Deuteronomy Chapters XI-XVI]

BERESHIT   SHEMOT   VAYIKRA   BAMIDBAR   **DEVARIM**   Baal Haturim
Devarim Vaetchanan Ekev **Reeh** Shoftim Ki Tetze Ki Tavo Nitzavim Vayelech Haazinu Vezot Habracha

The Metaphysics of Charity

There never was a person who did anything worth doing, who did not receive more than he gave. -Henry Ward Beecher

Being charitable is a Jewish value that is recorded already from the stories of our Patriarch Abraham. In the time of Moses it is codified as law, including the requirement to tithe. The Rabbis give further clarification as to the percentage and measurements of different agricultural donations that each farmer was expected to contribute.

The Baal Haturim on this week's Torah portion provides a number of pointers as to the metaphysical reality of charity. He states in Deuteronomy 12:19 that the act of giving charity leads directly to increased wealth. In Deuteronomy 15:8 he explains that if a person listens to and provides for the poor, God in turn will listen to and provide for the charitable person. The inverse is also true. If a person ignores the plea of the poor, God is likely to ignore the potentially charitable person.

Finally, the Baal Haturim on Deuteronomy 15:10 details that we should be careful to provide the solicitant what they need. He brings as an example the story of King David who when he was seeking refuge from the ire of King Saul escaped to the Cohanic city of Nov where they provided him with bread and a sword, two things he was in dire need of.

May we have the capacity and opportunity to be generous to those in need and may we see our generosity divinely and abundantly rewarded.

Dedication
To Rachel and Shalom Berger on their abundant celebrations.

BERESHIT SHEMOT VAYIKRA BAMIDBAR **DEVARIM** Netziv
Devarim Vaetchanan Ekev **Reeh** Shoftim Ki Tetze Ki Tavo Nitzavim Vayelech Haazinu Vezot Habracha

Inseparable Pair
"There is one evident, indubitable manifestation of the Divinity, and that is the laws of right which are made known to the world through Revelation." -Leo Tolstoy

The Bible details and repeats the account of the divine revelation of God to the entire people of Israel, where He, in His Awesomeness, speaks the famous Ten Commandments in front of the multitude of the Jewish nation who heard and accepted and survived the direct and powerful encounter with God. The giving of the commandments at Mount Sinai was probably the most extraordinary moment in all of human history.

However, Jewish tradition tells us that much more than ten commandments were conveyed at Sinai. In fact, the entire corpus of what we know as the Five Books of Moses, including all 613 commandments were transmitted directly to Moses at Sinai. Moses painstaking writes down, verbatim, the words of God to the world.

Yet there is even more. The Netziv on Deuteronomy 12:1 explains that not only was the Written Torah given to Moses at Sinai, but also the Oral Torah was delivered. There is an entire field of knowledge, much more expansive, deeper, filled with mysteries and secrets, that was given over to Moses during his personal encounter with God. The Oral Torah explains the Written Torah. The Oral Torah is inseparable from the Written Torah. The Written Torah cannot be understood, and in places does not make sense, without the explanations of the Oral Torah.

While it is true that the Written Torah is a fundamental, sacred document for us, it is just one part of the puzzle. It is incomplete, even defective, when studied alone, without the complementary Oral Torah. Parts of the Oral Torah were eventually committed to writing. The process started around 2,000 years ago with the Mishna, followed a few centuries later with the Talmud and subsequently with the written codes of law and rabbinic commentaries and explanations.

Both the Written and Oral Torah are our tradition. If we are to embrace our tradition, we should do so fully, completely, understanding it holistically, keeping the inseparable pair united.

Dedication
To the new banim and bnot sherut (young volunteer teachers from Israel) that have arrived in Montevideo. May they have much success in transmitting our written and oral traditions and having a positive impact on our community.

BERESHIT SHEMOT VAYIKRA BAMIDBAR **DEVARIM** Ibn Ezra
Devarim Vaetchanan Ekev **Reeh** Shoftim Ki Tetze Ki Tavo Nitzavim Vayelech Haazinu Vezot Habracha

Divine Entrapment

"One must be aware that one is continually being tested in what one wishes most in order to make clear whether one's heart is on earth or in heaven." -Pir Vilayat Khan

The Bible presents a thorny theological issue with the case of a false prophet. The false prophet is someone, usually charismatic, eloquent and powerful who may have the ability to read divine signs and even foretell the future. He would seem to be someone with the authority of God, but there is something off about him, something that just doesn't add up.

The false prophet changes something. It may be a little thing, it may seem inconsequential. What the false prophet changes is the law. He reinterprets the Law of Moses against the structure and tradition of the sages. We don't know his reasons, but the bottom line is that he is wrong.

How can God allow a being such as a false prophet to exist? How can God bless an individual with prophetic ability that will mislead the people of Israel from their faith, beliefs, traditions and rules?

Ibn Ezra on Deuteronomy 13:4 explains very simply, based on the verses, that God sends the false prophet to test us. He wishes to test us and demonstrate that we overcome. We should not be swayed by the charismatic leader. We should not be fooled by holy charlatans. We should not be tricked by apparently divine signs. We need to think for ourselves. We need to understand the laws and traditions and not rely on magical incantations or otherworldly promises. We must remain strong in our faith, in the unbroken traditions and the chain of law that has kept us as a people to this very day.

May we see tests of faith for what they are and pass them with flying colors.

Dedication

To all of the people who guided us in our voyage to Buenos Aires. They were each true prophets that led us to a wonderful trip and fantastic food.

BERESHIT SHEMOT VAYIKRA BAMIDBAR **DEVARIM** Ohr Hachayim
Devarim Vaetchanan Ekev **Reeh** Shoftim Ki Tetze Ki Tavo Nitzavim Vayelech Haazinu Vezot Habracha

Prophetic Frauds
"The wisest prophets make sure of the event first." -Horace Walpole

In the summer of 1503, over the course of his fourth and last voyage, Christopher Columbus and his crew found themselves stranded on the island of Jamaica. His ships were damaged by a major storm and no help was forthcoming. After six months of native hospitality, Columbus' crewmen had overstayed their welcome and the locals refused to provide the Europeans with any more food.

Though he was out of provisions, Columbus had in his possession the almanac of Regiomontaus which included astronomical tables for the years 1475-1506 with a listing of upcoming lunar eclipses. Columbus requested a meeting with the Cacique, the native leader, on the day of the expected full moon eclipse (March 1, 1504), when the Earth would block the sun from directly shining on the moon, thereby covering the moon with an unusual red tint. Columbus told the Cacique that God was upset with the treatment the Europeans were receiving, and that God would demonstrate His anger with a rising full moon "inflamed with wrath." Shortly thereafter the blood-colored moon filled the night sky to the horror of the natives. They begged and scurried to fulfill Admiral Columbus' every wish. Looking at his hourglass, Columbus announced that God would forgive them. When a few minutes later the eclipse receded, Columbus announced that they had indeed been forgiven. Thereafter, Columbus became a confirmed Prophet of God in the eyes of the local population.

Had Columbus pushed the locals to idol worship instead of providing much needed food, the Ohr Hachayim (based on Deuteronomy 13:2) might have simply killed Columbus for being a false prophet, even if his wondrous signs and predictions were fulfilled. Judaism is wary of prophets and predictions that carry an agenda that contravenes the Torah. It suspects such chicanery so much, that it gives the death penalty to whoever would fool his fellow into the path of strange worship, no matter how talented, insightful or "prophetic" they may be.

May we beware of false prophets and stick to simple faith without any magical side shows.

Dedication
To Edward Klitzler and his fascinating, engrossing, historical account: **Jewish Pirates of the Caribbean** – How a Generation of Swashbuckling Jews Carved Out an Empire in the New World in Their Quest for Treasure, Religious Freedom – and Revenge.

שופטים

Shoftim

[Deuteronomy Chapters XVI-XXI]

BERESHIT SHEMOT VAYIKRA BAMIDBAR **DEVARIM** Baal Haturim
Devarim Vaetchanan Ekev Reeh **Shoftim** Ki Tetze Ki Tavo Nitzavim Vayelech Haazinu Vezot Habracha

Lions of Judah

There is something behind the throne greater than the King himself. – William Pitt, The Elder Chatham

The Bible itself as well as subsequent Rabbinic commentators have mixed feelings regarding a monarchy. On one hand it seems to be a command that the nation of Israel should have a king. On the other hand, it seems that a monarchy may only be established if the nation desires one. If the nation wants a king, then there are certain guidelines as to the qualifications of a king as well as what he can and cannot do.

Not much after the nation of Israel conquers the land of Israel, we have the death of Joshua and the loss of centralized leadership. That time period is known biblically as the era of the Judges when over the course of a few hundred years the nation of Israel descends into civil war, chaos and anarchy. However, with the subsequent establishment of the monarchy of Israel, we relatively quickly get to corruption, idolatry and oppression, and a few hundred years after that, destruction and exile. In the long term, the difference between not having a monarchy and having one seems to be the difference between social madness and organized social madness.

Nonetheless, the Bible gives a tremendous amount of respect and importance to the historical monarchy. The desire for a king and the need to follow one to the people's liking is the source of much drama in the biblical books of Samuel and Kings and leads to the schism between the southern tribes (Judah and Benjamin) that remained loyal to the House of David and the ten northern tribes that went through various non-Davidic rulers. The Baal Haturim on Deuteronomy 17:15 points out to us that the kings of Israel are meant to be descendants of the tribe of "Lions", the tribe of Judah (as David, Salomon and their descendants were – and would indicate the northern tribes were ostensibly in the wrong in following non-Judean rulers, despite God's command and repeated intervention in the election (and assassination) of the kings of the ten tribes).

The error of non-Judean kings was repeated again during the second Temple era after the Hasmonean Revolt, where the successful Maccabees took the helm of political leadership despite being a Cohanic non-Judean family. The initial victory turned to ashes generations later as the Hasmonean line became corrupt and ends with Herod, who while an impressive builder, was a greater enemy of the Jewish people.

May we merit leadership of noble traits and correct pedigree, be they kings or otherwise.

BERESHIT   SHEMOT   VAYIKRA   BAMIDBAR   **DEVARIM**   Baal Haturim
Devarim Vaetchanan Ekev Reeh **Shoftim** *Ki Tetze Ki Tavo Nitzavim Vayelech Haazinu Vezot Habracha*

Dedication

To the two lions who included Montevideo in their courageous Halachic Adventures: Dr. Ari Greenspan and Rabbi Ari Zivotofsky.

BERESHIT   SHEMOT   VAYIKRA   BAMIDBAR   **DEVARIM**   Netziv
Devarim Vaetchanan Ekev Reeh **Shoftim** *Ki Tetze Ki Tavo Nitzavim Vayelech Haazinu Vezot Habracha*

Monarchical Vacillation

"No one pretends that democracy is perfect or all wise. Indeed, it has been said that democracy is the worst form of Government except all those other forms that have been tried from time to time." -Sir Winston Churchill, Speech in the House of Commons, November 11, 1947

The Bible seems to be of two minds when it comes to the topic of Monarchy. On one hand it appears to be a command, that the people of Israel should appoint a king to rule them. On the other hand, both in God's messages to the people, and as we have seen throughout history – a king is more often than not a greater curse for his subjects than a blessing.

When trying to imagine a Messianic future, there are some as well that picture the return of the Monarchy. It is prophesied that a descendant of King David will rule Israel, but will it be as King, as some benevolent tyrant, or will his powers be circumscribed by some other government institutions creating a balance of power?

The Netziv on Deuteronomy 17:14 explains that the commandment to appoint a king is an optional one. It is only if the people desire and demand a king. If there is a king in place, then the Torah provides certain guidelines, restrictions and privileges for the king. But it is not a necessity for Israel to have a monarch. It is perfectly permissible for the people of Israel to choose some other form of government for self-rule. It can even be a democracy.

May we improve the governing institutions we have and be grateful that they are not worse.

Dedication

To our elected officials in all their functions and capacities. May God bless them, give them wisdom, compassion and good judgment.

BERESHIT SHEMOT VAYIKRA BAMIDBAR **DEVARIM**   Ibn Ezra
Devarim Vaetchanan Ekev Reeh **Shoftim** Ki Tetze Ki Tavo Nitzavim Vayelech Haazinu Vezot Habracha

"Don't do me any favors"

"No matter how small and unimportant what we are doing may seem, if we do it well, it may soon become the step that will lead us to better things." -Channing Pollock

Probably one of the worst displays of helpfulness is the half-hearted assistance. Someone offers to do the dishes. You are relieved by the sudden, unexpected and generous help. Your vital time is freed up to tend to other pressing matters. But the person who did the dishes, didn't really want to do them. It was a mock kindness, a weary, lazy effort pretending to be helpful, perhaps even just seeking the claim of helpfulness, but really merely fulfilling a self-serving desire to proclaim to the world the righteousness of the impromptu dishwasher.

You return to the dishes and notice that there is a ring of hardened dirt on one, a splotch of dried grease on another, a discoloration that just won't come off on the third. You now attack the dishes yourself with more energy, force and frustration than you would have without the Good Samaritan's help. It is probably from such a fear of the unenthused offers of help that the phrase "Don't do me any favors" was born, (I traced it to the Yiddish: *"Ti mir nit kayn toyves"*).

God has a similar attitude when it comes to certain aspects of our worship of Him, especially in the more voluntary commandments. Ibn Ezra on Deuteronomy 17:1 highlights this on the prohibition of bringing a blemished animal as a sacrifice. He explains that it is better not to bring anything than to bring a blemished animal. It's as if God is saying "Don't do me any favors – if you can't be bothered to bring me a pristine animal, if you can't be bothered to do the commandment properly – don't do it at all."

It must be noted that this is a rare view in the performance of commandments. A more general philosophy is that even if someone performs a commandment imperfectly, he should continue, in the hopes and expectations that he will eventually learn to do it properly. However, on some matters, especially where we can clearly do better – God may take umbrage at a lackadaisical attitude.

May we work harder on the simple things within our reach – they count as well.

Dedication

To the Jewish community of Punta del Este. It's a summer destination with year-round warmth.

BERESHIT SHEMOT VAYIKRA BAMIDBAR **DEVARIM** Ohr Hachayim
Devarim Vaetchanan Ekev Reeh **Shoftim** *Ki Tetze Ki Tavo Nitzavim Vayelech Haazinu Vezot Habracha*

Every Man A City

"Man: The most complex of beings, and thus the most dependent of beings. On all that made you up, you depend." -Andre Gide

Plato's Republic (circa 380 BCE) is considered the first text in our possession to compare a human being to a city. The parallels are many. We are composed of many different parts. We have many requirements. We have different elements vying for attention. Despite the different parts and demands, they need to get along harmoniously, there needs to be an internal balance, otherwise the entity ceases to function.

Plato goes on to compare the citizens of a city to the soul of a person, with its own divisions. The Ohr Hachayim however, draws parallel lessons from even earlier sources: *"When thou drawest nigh unto a city to fight against it, then proclaim peace unto it."* Deuteronomy 20:10 (circa 1,300 BCE), as well as from Solomon's Kohelet 9:14 (Ecclesiastes) (circa 800 BCE).

Based on the sources, The Ohr Hachayim compares a Canaanite city to a person under the sway of the Evil Inclination, while the attacking Israelites are the Good Inclination trying to wrest control of the person. The Ohr Hachayim explains that a direct frontal assault will not work. The Good Inclination needs to call out "peace" to the Evil Inclination and reach some areas of understanding. The Evil Inclination needs to understand some of the benefits of a noble lifestyle and to allow some of the baser instincts such as eating and drinking to serve the purposes of the Good Inclination. Such an approach as opposed to head-on all-out war gives the complete city, the complete person, a greater chance of victory.

May we keep our personal cities in order and channel our different parts in the right direction.

Dedication

In Memory of Rabbi Avraham Chaim Roth (Rata) of blessed memory, Grand Rabbi of the Chasidic dynasty, the Shomrei Emunim. I have never met anyone with greater wisdom, saintliness and divine inspiration than the Admor of the Shomer Emunim. He had a great impact on my life and he will be sorely missed. May his memory be a blessing.

כי תצא

Ki Tetze

[Deuteronomy Chapters XXI-XXV]

BERESHIT SHEMOT VAYIKRA BAMIDBAR **DEVARIM** Baal Haturim
Devarim Vaetchanan Ekev Reeh Shoftim **Ki Tetze** Ki Tavo Nitzavim Vayelech Haazinu Vezot Habracha

Ugly Language

The foolish and wicked practice of profane cursing and swearing is a vice so mean and low that every person of sense and character detests and despises it. -George Washington

One of the most defining characteristics of human beings are their ability to speak. And in a sense, the words we use define us, but not only the words that come out of our mouths, but also the words that we hear, the words that infuse our being. And in that area, like in so many others, we have free choice. We can choose both what to speak and what to hear. There are few situations where we are forced either to say something or to listen to something.

The Baal Haturim on Deuteronomy 23:14 warns about this matter and specifically about "nivul pe", literally "the disgustingness of the mouth". He states clearly and simply that if we suddenly find ourselves exposed to foul language, to things that are not appropriate to be spoken, we should simply stick our fingers in our ears or get up and leave.

We would not subject ourselves (or our children) to harmful fumes, substances or dangerous situations. The same is true regarding foul language. It is toxic, corrupting and disgusting. The fact that it is widely used and accepted by the masses does not make it any better. Do not accept it. Do not stand for it. Let it be known that you disapprove. You will be surprised by the positive reactions people will have to this small stand of principle. And if they don't get it, spend your time with more refined people.

Dedication

To the incoming class of Midreshet and Yeshivat Torah V'Avodah. I expect you will hear many beautiful words from your teachers and administration.

Foolish Friends

"Don't approach a goat from the front, a horse from the back, or a fool from any side." -Yiddish Proverb

Human foolishness comes in all shapes and sizes. No person is completely immune from foolish acts, though most of us generally try to avoid doing or saying things we will later regret. Animals on the other hand function almost exclusively on instinct; there are rarely situations in the course of nature in which an animal would be called foolish.

However, in Jewish law, there is a term, typically used for bulls, called "muad". Muad translates as either notorious or prone to do damage and is a label assigned to an animal that has proven itself to be dangerous, based on past attempts to gore. The owner of a Muad animal is liable for all damages, while a previously tranquil animal has a lower level of liability for the owner.

Men are in a completely different category. They are always considered dangerous. Man is always considered Muad. He is always prone and responsible for damages that he causes his fellow man. The Netziv on Deuteronomy 24:9 fine-tunes this concept even further and states that a person is Muad, even in sins that he commits against another unintentionally.

Meaning, a person is responsible for the damage caused by a completely innocent act or remark, even if there was no harm intended. This gives us a tremendous level of responsibility for what we do and say. We are still guilty of unintended consequences. We must know better. We must think ahead. We must realize the power we have as humans to affect those around us. It is a serious power.

May we use our human capacities well, with foresight and intelligence and avoid both fools and foolishness.

Dedication

To the conversion class of Montevideo. Good luck on your upcoming tests!

BERESHIT SHEMOT VAYIKRA BAMIDBAR **DEVARIM**   Ibn Ezra
Devarim Vaetchanan Ekev Reeh Shoftim **Ki Tetze** Ki Tavo Nitzavim Vayelech Haazinu
Vezot Habracha

Foundations for Life

"If we do not maintain Justice, Justice will not maintain us." -Francis Bacon

In the period approaching the New Year and Yom Kippur, one may wonder as to the preponderance of concern with Divine Justice. If as we believe, God is also merciful, then why the excessive concern with the aspect of justice? Can't He just go easy with us and understand that man (whom He created) inevitably sins? How can He demand that everyone behave with integrity, how can He expect everyone to uphold justice in a world filled with deceit and injustice?

Ibn Ezra on Deuteronomy 25:15 explains that justice is not only a Divine attribute but that it is also a requirement of the human condition. Man cannot live long or well without the aspect of justice, of fairness, of evenhandedness as a basic element of his existence.

Ibn Ezra compares justice in man to the foundations of a building. If we chip away at the foundations, the building will eventually collapse. If man erodes his sense of justice, of integrity, of honesty, Ibn Ezra alludes that eventually such a person will also collapse and perhaps that his existence will even end earlier than it might have.

May we stand on guard for the erosion of our principles, may we reinforce the elements of integrity and fairness in our lives and may we prepare ourselves for the upcoming High Holidays so that the structure of our lives may endure and prosper.

Dedication

To the communications team of the Kehila for their heroic and ongoing efforts in preparation of the High Holidays.

In memory of Ivan Porzecanski (Natan ben Rachel ve Rafael), a boy of three, for whom I had the heartbreaking duty of burying. May his family be consoled amongst the mourners of Zion and Jerusalem.

BERESHIT SHEMOT VAYIKRA BAMIDBAR **DEVARIM** Ohr Hachayim
Devarim Vaetchanan Ekev Reeh Shoftim **Ki Tetze** Ki Tavo Nitzavim Vayelech Haazinu Vezot Habracha

Individual Torah

"Never forget that you are one of a kind. Never forget that if there weren't any need for you in all your uniqueness to be on this earth, you wouldn't be here in the first place. And never forget, no matter how overwhelming life's challenges and problems seem to be, that one person can make a difference in the world. In fact, it is always because of one person that all the changes that matter in the world come about. So be that one person." -Richard Buckminster Fuller

When one finally gets the enormity of what the Torah encompasses, it can be fairly overwhelming: The Bible, Mishna, Talmud, all of their ancient and modern commentaries, Jewish Law, Philosophy, Ethics, History and more. The list is enormous, with more material being added every day. It is no wonder it is called a "sea of Torah" – one can drown by being immersed in so much information.

Nonetheless, we are enjoined to study it. To start slowly, even superficially, but to start. To start and to continue. The Ohr Hachayim adds another dimension to this command, one that is reflected in the Silent Prayer of the Sabbath where we beseech of God "to give us **our** part in your Torah".

The Ohr Hachayim on Deuteronomy 22:3 assigns three components to man: the body, the soul and man's unique portion of the Torah. He explains that every single Jew has their own individual part of the Torah that they need to find and connect with. There is some otherworldly component; independent even of the soul, which is comparable to man's missing rib. Man needs to find that Torah portion that only he can uncover, that only he can bring to light, absorb it, refine it and make it his.

May we all find our unique parts of the Torah and share them with the world.

Dedication

To all the students immersing themselves in Torah with the beginning of the school year. We look forward to each unique contribution.

כי תבוא

Ki Tavo

[Deuteronomy Chapters XXVI-XXIX]

BERESHIT SHEMOT VAYIKRA BAMIDBAR **DEVARIM**   Baal Haturim
Devarim Vaetchanan Ekev Reeh Shoftim Ki Tetze **Ki Tavo** *Nitzavim Vayelech Haazinu Vezot Habracha*

Respect the Silence

Men are respectable only as they respect. -Ralph Waldo Emerson

I've noticed that the volume in a room is often in direct proportion to the comfort the people in the room feel. Parties can be unbearably loud. Cemeteries are appropriately quiet. However, there are multiple occasions where quiet is both expected and given. Official assemblies of all sorts will have their moments of quiet.

Synagogue prayer is a conundrum. On one hand, we want participants to be happy and comfortable. For many it is a great opportunity to catch up with friends, to relax and chat. However, we are also supposed to be there to pray to God.

Jewish law is unequivocal about talking during prayer – it is forbidden, besides being rude, insensitive, ego-centric and disturbing. Our sages went so far as to institute a special prayer bestowing great blessings upon those who are careful not to speak in the synagogue.

The Baal Haturim on Deuteronomy 26:19 takes things a step further. He explains that when one is focused on his prayer, it is as if he is constructing a crown made out of prayers which is then placed, as it were, upon God's head. However, subsequently, in some spiritual, mystical sense, that crown then returns to the prayerful person. However, those who instead of respecting the prayerful quiet choose instead to talk during the services, instead of receiving a divine crown, they will be punished. The punishment, states the Baal Haturim, is that they will receive thorns all over their body.

May chatter in the synagogue be diminished and may we be spared from any punishments.

Dedication

To all the participants in the Maimonides Shabbaton. Thank you for a great Shabbaton and for quiet and meaningful prayers.

BERESHIT SHEMOT VAYIKRA BAMIDBAR **DEVARIM** Netziv
Devarim Vaetchanan Ekev Reeh Shoftim Ki Tetze **Ki Tavo** *Nitzavim Vayelech Haazinu Vezot Habracha*

Cosmetic Beauty

"Beauty is not in the face; beauty is a light in the heart." -Kahlil Gibran

In the Western, Greek-inspired world youth has become synonymous with beauty. To look younger is to be beautiful. To that end, it has become growingly popular to alter ones appearance, even via surgery, to achieve the elusive façade of eternal youth.

Judaism has an opposite view regarding youth and beauty. Old age and hard-earned wrinkles are to be venerated. Outward beauty is often false, deceptive. The beauty of the soul is paramount.

In this week's Torah reading instructions are provided as to the construction of the altar: only whole stones can be used. The Netziv on Deuteronomy 27:6 explains that the stones for the altar cannot be cut into more convenient or pleasing shapes. The natural stone must be used as is, without alterations or cosmetic surgery. The right stones need to be found and need to be used together with whatever blemishes or imperfections they have, without smoothing them, without cutting them. They are perfect and pleasing and wanted as they were created, in order to build the altar to God.

May we be comfortable with our own superficial blemishes and work instead on our inner beauty.

Dedication

To the five beautiful couples that married this week in one unforgettable night. May the beauty you find in each other only grow over time.

BERESHIT SHEMOT VAYIKRA BAMIDBAR **DEVARIM** Ibn Ezra
Devarim Vaetchanan Ekev Reeh Shoftim Ki Tetze **Ki Tavo** Nitzavim Vayelech Haazinu Vezot Habracha

Secret Sins

"The secret thoughts of a man run over all things, holy, profane, clean, obscene, grave, and light, without shame or blame." -Thomas Hobbes

There is a special place in Jewish theology for the secret sinner. He is cursed like few others are cursed. Moses commands the people of Israel to perform an unusual ceremony once they cross the Jordan River into the Promised Land.

Half the tribes of Israel are to stand on one mountain and half on the opposite mountain as they scream at each other curses into the air. The selection and content of the curses is unusual. For example: Cursed is the one who makes a secret idol. Cursed is the one who hits his parents. Cursed is the one who is intimate with a relative. Cursed is the one who confuses the blind on the road. (See the full list in Deuteronomy 27:15-26).

Ibn Ezra on Deuteronomy 27:14 explains that the common denominator between all the curses is that they are cursing those who perform sins in secret. One may be a respected, righteous figure on the outside and none know of the secret sin, (not that it's better to start sinning publicly!) – but this saintly figure starts living a dual existence. A monstrous Dr. Jekyll and Mr. Hyde with the secret sin eroding and poisoning the persona from the inside.

Only by breaking free of the secret sin can a person hope to be whole again.

Good luck to all of us.

Dedication

To all of us contemplating repentance of our sins, whether secret or less so. We are all invited to synagogue for the High Holidays.

BERESHIT SHEMOT VAYIKRA BAMIDBAR **DEVARIM** Ohr Hachayim
Devarim Vaetchanan Ekev Re'eh Shoftim Ki Tetze **Ki Tavo** Nitzavim Vayelech Haazinu Vezot Habracha

Soul Hijackers

Restlessness is discontent and discontent is the first necessity of progress. Show me a thoroughly satisfied man and I will show you a failure. -Thomas Alva Edison

There is comfort in the status quo. You may not always like it, but it is predictable, it is safe. Change requires risk. There is danger. The results may even be worse than what you've become accustomed to.

Therefore, I am often surprised and even amazed by people who change their circumstances: a brooding personality who tackles a new project with zest; a person that takes on an entirely new career; and in recent years, I've been astonished by people who would have never dreamed of Aliyah (immigration to Israel) yet suddenly find themselves living in the Promised Land, in total contravention to their personality, plans or expectations.

The Ohr Hachayim (on Deuteronomy 26:8) may provide a hint as to why people might do positive things, seemingly almost against their nature. He claims that every soul has an obligation to fulfill all of the commandments. However, this is typically impossible. There are commands that can only be fulfilled by women, others that can only be fulfilled by men, some can only be done by a Kohen, a significant portion can only be done when the Temple stands in Jerusalem, and many can only be done in the Land of Israel.

What is a lacking soul to do, that did not manage to perform all the commands during its lifetime? Simple. It hitches a ride on a living person that has the capacity to do the command they missed out on. This ghostly soul hangs about our living carrier and may even gently nudge or persuade the unsuspecting person to do its bidding. That way it racks up its commandments count. (How many souls can attach themselves to a person? How do they choose a person? How much influence do they really have? What if they choose the wrong horse? Can they hop off and choose someone more promising? What about the commands that we still can't do? Is there a waiting area for all those unfulfilled souls? Lots of questions on this whole concept...)

For millennia, Jews were unable to perform the commandments that depended on the Land of Israel. Finally we are able to. Is it any surprise then that people feel that tug to come to Israel and somehow, almost against their will, find themselves arriving at Ben-Gurion Airport?

What souls are hanging around you, where do they want to take you, and what are they whispering to you to do?

BERESHIT SHEMOT VAYIKRA BAMIDBAR **DEVARIM** Ohr Hachayim
Devarim Vaetchanan Ekev Reeh Shoftim Ki Tetze **Ki Tavo** Nitzavim Vayelech Haazinu Vezot Habracha

Dedication

To the marriages of Yakira Wiesel to Michael Azulay and of Michal Shimoni to Ronen Paz. May the souls of each new couple intertwine and may they know bliss, happiness and much joy in their new directions.

נצבים

Nitzavim

[Deuteronomy Chapters XXIX-XXX]

BERESHIT SHEMOT VAYIKRA BAMIDBAR **DEVARIM**   Baal Haturim
Devarim Vaetchanan Ekev Reeh Shoftim Ki Tetze Ki Tavo **Nitzavim** *Vayelech Haazinu Vezot Habracha*

Instant Global Cure

To reform a world, to reform a nation, no wise man will undertake; and all but foolish men know, that the only solid, though a far slower reformation, is what each begins and perfects on himself. -Thomas Carlyle

We are drowning in a sea of strife and pain. Wherever we look, whatever we read, we cannot avoid the disrespect, the insensitivity, the cruelty, and the mayhem of one human being to another.

One common reaction is to sigh a breath of resignation. I am too far away. I am too small. I am too insignificant to affect this fight. Another reaction is to complain. To curse the powers that be and all those who stand aside, as evils are committed uncontested.

There is a third, slower path, one that doesn't necessarily fix the suffering staring us in the face, not completely nor immediately. But it is a step. That path is called repentance.

The Baal Haturim on Deuteronomy 30:8 talks about repentance. We must first find what is wrong in us and fix it. If there is disrespect, insensitivity or cruelty in us, we must address it before we can presume to lecture others. However, the Baal Haturim states something surprising. He explains that if we can achieve complete repentance we shall see and experience immediate redemption.

May we strive for full repentance on a personal, familiar, communal and global basis.

Dedication

To Rabbi Asher Weiss, a wise man.

Personal and Group Judgment

There is a destiny that makes us brothers, No one goes his way alone; All that we send into the lives of others, Comes back into our own. -Edwin Markham

Jewish prayer consists of both personal pleas and communal orations. The liturgy itself also reflects this duality of seeking the welfare of the individual as well as of the group. The question however, for the High Holidays, is whether this dichotomy continues. Are we judged for our personal faults or are there also some accounting of group sins, and if so, how does that work?

The Netziv on Deuteronomy 29:9 digs into the issue and comes to the following conclusions. We are primarily judged as individuals, and not in comparison to others. We are judged based on our own personal potential, on what we could have achieved and didn't, on what we could have avoided but instead gave in to temptation. Each person has their own unique scale of accomplishments and that is what God looks at.

However, just as a person has their own particular attributes and potential, groups likewise have attributes and potential and God judges the aggregate of the people that make up particular groups, whether it is a family unit, a company, a school, a synagogue, a community, a city, a country or a people. If groups live up to their potential they are duly rewarded – and if they don't, then their *raison d'être* comes into question. Each group has its own unique mission that only they can achieve.

May we take the opportunity of the New Year, not only to evaluate ourselves, but also all the different groups we are a part of, and plan on a year where we live our unique potentials and missions both for ourselves and together with all those who we are connected to.

Dedication

To all the groups that I am a part of. I beg forgiveness of you for my errors, shortcomings and faults.

"That could never happen to me"

"A man is his own easiest dupe, for what he wishes to be true he generally believes to be true." –Demosthenes

There is a macabre curiosity in the suffering of others. The most vivid example is the traffic jams that occur on the opposite lane of a car accident. People slow down, not necessarily to see if they could help, but out of a deep desire to witness the misfortune of the other guy.

We feel a brief pang of empathy for the victims of the tragedy, remind ourselves to perhaps fasten our seatbelt or drive slower or more carefully, and then cruise on at the same speed, saying to ourselves that we would never be so careless or so unfortunate as the person being wheeled into the ambulance.

Ibn Ezra on Deuteronomy 29:18 says that man does the same mental calculation upon hearing the curses and punishments that God will bring upon those that don't follow His commandments. The foolhardy man will bless himself saying "that curse, that punishment, won't fall upon me." And he will believe his self-blessing to be true and effective though he may be obliviously careening into the approaching misfortune with his name written all over it.

May we wake up to reality from our self-delusions and get back onto safer and more honest roads.

Dedication

To Ana Duschitz on her incredible hosting of the Women's Weekly shiur of Montevideo. May it continue strongly in the coming year and grow.

BERESHIT   SHEMOT   VAYIKRA   BAMIDBAR   **DEVARIM**   Ohr Hachayim
Devarim Vaetchanan Ekev Reeh Shoftim Ki Tetze Ki Tavo **Nitzavim** *Vayelech Haazinu Vezot Habracha*

The Worst Curse
"Memory is the scribe of the soul." -Aristotle

Judaism ascribes much meaning and power to words. This coming week, as we celebrate the Jewish New Year, there is a tradition at the meal to pronounce blessings for the coming year, as well as curses calling for the destruction of our enemies. Jews have not lacked for enemies or colorful curses to bestow upon them.

One of my earliest introductions to Yiddish was the imaginative curse: "May you grow like an onion, with your head in the ground and feet in the air." (*Vaksn zolstu vi a tsibele mitn kop in dr'erd un di fis farkert!*) However, the worst curse used by the Jews is the phrase "Erased shall be his name and his memory." (*Yemach shemo ve'zicroh*).

One can think of much more graphic, violent, demeaning curses than what might seem like an innocuous wish for someone to be forgotten. However, the curse of erasure is reserved exclusively for the most horrific villains in the history of Judaism.

The Ohr Hachayim (on Deuteronomy 29:19) explains why this might be so. Erasure, he describes, is nothing less than the cutting off of a soul. Every human has a soul. That soul is a divine spark, the eternal part of his being, his personality, that will survive long after his body has turned to dust. To have ones soul cut off means the destruction of that eternal soul, it means the removal of the divine element in man. It means that when the person dies, there is no hereafter. It is pure oblivion. It is the destruction of an immortal being. It is considered the worst punishment imaginable, worse than all the suffering of this world or the next.

The flip side is that barring such a horrific destiny, we all possess a part of God within us, that under normal circumstances will connect us to Him forever. He wants us to nourish the soul, protect it, grow it and return it better than how He gave it to us. The coming week is considered particularly timely for introspection as to how we've been treating our soul this year and what strategies we might pursue to improve our performance in the coming year.

May we all have a year inscribed for blessing, good memories, health, happiness and great success.

Dedication
To all those that I may have harmed, offended, annoyed or in any way disturbed – I ask your forgiveness – and your blessings.

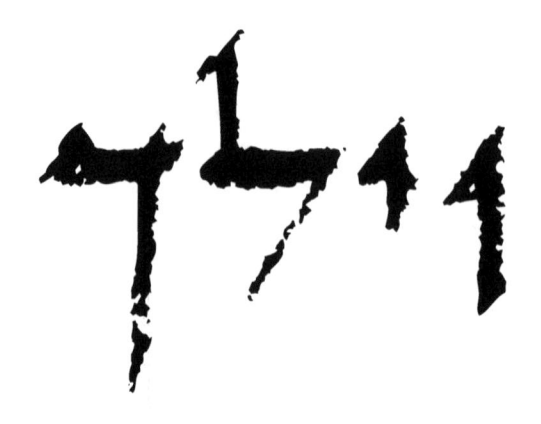

Vayelech

[Deuteronomy Chapter XXXI]

BERESHIT SHEMOT VAYIKRA BAMIDBAR **DEVARIM** Baal Haturim
Devarim Vaetchanan Ekev Reeh Shoftim Ki Tetze Ki Tavo Nitzavim **Vayelech** *Haazinu Vezot Habracha*

Afterlife Conversations

We talk about heaven being so far away. It is within speaking distance to those who belong there. Heaven is a prepared place for a prepared people. -Dwight L. Moody

For good reason, there is great uncertainty about the afterlife. I have yet to meet someone who has been there and back, who could give a personal account of what it was like. Some doubt its existence as there is no scientific proof. Others may believe in various Hollywood versions, inspired in part from classical poets like Dante and Milton.

The Jewish tradition has much to say about the next world. What's its purpose, who gets there and who doesn't, what do we do there, how long we're there for, and much more.

The Baal Haturim points out an interesting capability we will retain in the afterlife. In his commentary on Deuteronomy 31:1, he cites a conversation between Moses and the Patriarchs (Abraham, Isaac and Jacob), whereby Moses informs them that God has fulfilled his centuries-old promise to them, that their descendents, the Children of Israel, have finally inherited the Land of Israel. The Baal Haturim explains that the above account is the source that the dead talk to each other in the next world.

May our patriarchs and ancestors have good things to say about us, especially as we approach the Day of Judgment.

Dedication

To the Chazan, Shaul Hochberger, on his divine conversations leading our prayers.

BERESHIT SHEMOT VAYIKRA BAMIDBAR **DEVARIM** Ohr Hachayim
Devarim Vaetchanan Ekev Re'eh Shoftim Ki Tetze Ki Tavo Nitzavim **Vayelech** Haazinu
Vezot Habracha

Instant Repentance

"Any man worth his salt will stick up for what he believes right, but it takes a slightly better man to acknowledge instantly and without reservation that he is in error." -General Peyton C. March

We are a generation obsessed with instant gratification. Instant coffee, instant noodles, instant camera, instant messenger, instant relationships. If you can think of it, you can demand it and expect it, instantly.

In general, Judaism has a dim view of things occurring instantly. We teach our children to obey the commandments, so that when they are finally obligated to perform them years later, they are familiar with them. We believe in daily, weekly, yearly consistent service. We believe in hard work and perseverance that will lead you to goals and achievement.

However, there are at least two areas where Judaism believes that things can occur in an instant. The first is redemption. The prophets and the Rabbis have written extensively how redemption can come "in the blink of an eye." In fact, we await the Messianic redemption every day, in whatever form it will eventually take.

The second and perhaps related "instant" phenomenon in Judaism is repentance.

In one of his parting speeches, Moses castigates the Children of Israel, as follows:

"For I know your rebellion, and your stiff neck; behold, while I am yet alive with you this day, you **were** *rebellious against the Lord; and how much more after my death?"* -Deuteronomy 31:27

The Ohr Hachayim picks up on the fact that Moses speaks of the rebelliousness of the Children of Israel of that very day as being in the past which is furthermore not consistent with the other tenses in the verse.

The Ohr Hachayim explains that Moses' change of tense is purposeful and that his addressing their up-until-now rebelliousness as a thing of the past is an indication of Israel's potentially immediate repentance.

The Ohr Hachayim further quotes the Talmud (Tractate Kiddushin 49b):

"Whoever marries a woman on condition that he is completely righteous, even though we know him to be completely bad, the marriage is binding as he may have repented during that instant."

How's that for instant results?

May we achieve repentance in any way and timeframe we can.

BERESHIT SHEMOT VAYIKRA BAMIDBAR **DEVARIM**   *Ohr Hachayim*
Devarim Vaetchanan Ekev Reeh Shoftim Ki Tetze Ki Tavo Nitzavim **Vayelech** Haazinu
Vezot Habracha

Dedication

To the entire Jewish people, as we stand in judgment during this period. May we thrive in the coming year and been given more opportunities to excel.

הַאֲזִינוּ

Haazinu

[Deuteronomy Chapter XXXII]

BERESHIT SHEMOT VAYIKRA BAMIDBAR **DEVARIM** Baal Haturim
Devarim Vaetchanan Ekev Reeh Shoftim Ki Tetze Ki Tavo Nitzavim Vayelech *Haazinu*
Vezot Habracha

Forging the Eternal Inheritance

A man cannot leave a better legacy to the world than a well-educated family. -Thomas Scott

It is my sober duty to bury the dead and console the living. It gives one ample opportunities to ponder the legacy people leave behind. The family matriarch who lived to see great-grandchildren following in her footsteps of kindness. The grandfather who was a well-known joke-teller with grandchildren who continue with the same entertaining sense of humor. Or those who died before they lived to see successive generations but left behind memories of strength and joy. Or those who left behind money and property to then be squabbled over by the children.

From a multi-generation, decades long perspective, it is sobering to consider what a parent should inculcate in their children, what they should hope to see in their grandchildren, what are the greatest gifts one can bestow on their progeny that will have a positive and lasting impact on ones descendants and on the world.

The Baal Haturim on Deuteronomy 32:7 sets the goal of Torah scholarship as the pinnacle of what a parent can hope for. He explains that if a family merits to see three successive generations of Torah scholars, that gift, that accomplishment becomes an eternal inheritance, for the family and for the wider nation of Israel.

One of the great scholars of the past was once asked, how many years did it take him to accumulate the vast knowledge of Torah that was at his fingertips. He answered: "Five minutes." The questioner looked at the scholar in confusion. The scholar explained: "Whenever I was at a bus stop, whenever I was standing on line, whenever I had five minutes free, I would learn. Those five minutes added up."

If our fathers were not great scholars, it does not exempt us from striving, nor from setting an example for our children and grandchildren. It just takes five minutes.

Dedication

To the *Chok Le'Israel*. A book that provides really bite-size daily servings of the spectrum of Torah. Very highly recommended.

BERESHIT SHEMOT VAYIKRA BAMIDBAR **DEVARIM** Netziv
Devarim Vaetchanan Ekev Re'eh Shoftim Ki Tetze Ki Tavo Nitzavim Vayelech *Haazinu* Vezot Habracha

Voodoo Judaism

It is superstitious to put one's hopes in formalities, but arrogant to refuse to submit to them. -Blaise Pascal

In Judaism, we have rituals and sacred objects. There is also a belief that performing these rituals and utilizing these objects can have a positive influence on our lives and world. However, if we limit ourselves to merely this method of operation, it is a shallow understanding of how the spiritual world interacts with our physical one.

It is not merely some sorcerous trick, that by putting the traditional *mezuza* by the door, that one's home will be protected. It is not slight-of-hand that determines that a person who gives a tenth of his income to charity will see financial success. It is not magic that the reciting of Psalms is known to give solace as well as influence the world around us.

However, when a person deficient in multiple aspects of their lives, blames their ill-fortune on the quality of their *mezuza*, then there is something wrong with their concept of Judaism, commandments and a relationship with God.

The Netziv on Deuteronomy 32:2 explains that these simpler, ritual commandments are good and have a positive influence on smaller things. But he clarifies that the ultimate benefit comes from hard-earned knowledge of the Torah, of God's laws and will in this world. That familiarity, when the Torah becomes a part of oneself, influences all other successes.

The little acts are good and important, but they are only the edges of a much vaster system of influences. At the heart of that system is the work and effort we put into understanding God's directives to us. His Torah. A connection to God via his laws is the ultimate guarantor of eternal success.

May we strengthen ourselves in this New Year to reacquaint ourselves with the rulebook, with the expectations God has of us, which in the end guarantees a deeper, more meaningful and more successful existence.

Dedication

To Misha Beshkin, creator of the "Is It Kosher?" app. He is facilitating the world's familiarity with Kosher products and has helped bring our Uruguayan list to wider use.

BERESHIT SHEMOT VAYIKRA BAMIDBAR **DEVARIM** Ibn Ezra
Devarim Vaetchanan Ekev Reeh Shoftim Ki Tetze Ki Tavo Nitzavim Vayelech **Haazinu**
Vezot Habracha

Beware the Four Horsemen

"I'm not afraid to die, I just don't want to be there when it happens." - Woody Allen

Death chases us all down like an implacable horseman; it is merely the time and the manner of the dying that is a variable. The famed Four Horsemen of Apocalypse or of Death are drawn from the verses of The New Testament, but there are earlier echoes of the concept in our Torah.

Ibn Ezra on Deuteronomy 32:24 draws our attention to what he calls the four agents of death: Famine, Plague, Wild Beasts and the Sword.

God sends these as a direct consequence for our wrongdoings, not to destroy the world, but as both personal and communal punishments for choosing the wrong path.

To be spared from these terrible endings the Torah suggests a very simple solution: Follow God's commandments. Let's take the opportunity of this Rosh Hashana to review the commandments we should be working on and reestablish that God is the boss.

Dedication

To the end of the year 5773 and to the beginning of 5774. May the new year be filled with all the wonderful blessings we hope for.

BERESHIT SHEMOT VAYIKRA BAMIDBAR **DEVARIM** Ohr Hachayim
Devarim Vaetchanan Ekev Reeh Shoftim Ki Tetze Ki Tavo Nitzavim Vayelech Haazinu
Vezot Habracha

Hearing-Aid for the Dead

"The voice of conscience is so delicate that it is easy to stifle it; but it is also so clear that it is impossible to mistake it." -Germaine De Stael

One of the cardinal beliefs of Judaism, as articulated by Maimonides in his thirteen principles of faith is that at some point in the future God will bring the dead back to life:

Principle 13: *"I believe with complete faith that there shall be a revival of the dead..."*

Who God will revive is another matter entirely, and there is great debate amongst Rabbis as far back as the Mishna (2,000 years ago) as to what qualifies someone for revival or not.

Moses, in his eloquent and final poetic prophecy to the Children of Israel states:

"Give ear, ye heavens, and I will speak; and let the earth hear the words of my mouth." -*Deuteronomy 32:1*

The Ohr Hachayim wonders what aspect of the earth Moses is addressing. He answers that Moses is speaking to none other than the dwellers of the earth, those buried there, namely, the dead.

The Ohr Hachayim explains very simply that if one heard God's voice, God's instructions, God's precepts while they were alive, they will hear God's voice again when he calls the dead from their slumber and they will awaken. If one was deaf during his lifetime to God's call, to God's whispering, to God's directives, then he is unlikely to hear Him when he calls again during the promised revival of the dead.

May we unclog our ears and our minds and listen to what God is telling us.

Dedication

To AV Israel. A worthy organization for hearing-impaired children in Israel.

וזאת הברכה

Vezot Habracha

[Deuteronomy Chapters XXXIII-XXXIV]

BERESHIT SHEMOT VAYIKRA BAMIDBAR **DEVARIM**   Baal Haturim
Devarim Vaetchanan Ekev Reeh Shoftim Ki Tetze Ki Tavo Nitzavim Vayelech Haazinu Vezot Habracha

Pre-Incarnated Unity

The soul gives unity to what it looks at with love. -Thomas Carlyle

At what was perhaps the most transcendent moment in human history, God reveals Himself to the Jewish people at Mount Sinai, where the Ten Commandments are uttered and God gives the remainder of the Written and Oral Torah to Moses. Every single one of the Children of Israel who was alive at that time, shortly after the Exodus from Egypt, hears and senses God at prophetic levels.

There follows a question as to how this bond, this covenant that was formed at Sinai can continue through the long generations and millennia since that singular event. What connects, what unites the descendants of those who stood at Sinai with the ancestors who witnessed the barely filtered presence of God?

Amongst many answers, a popular one is that the soul of every Jew was at Sinai, even if he hadn't been born yet. Somehow, at this defining event for the Jewish people, every Jewish soul, alive as well as unborn, through all the generations, was present for the receipt of the Torah, for the establishment of the everlasting covenant with God.

The Baal Haturim on Deuteronomy 33:3 adds another facet to this well known explanation. He elaborates that not only was the soul of every future Jew in history present at Sinai, but that even the souls of future converts were present at the encounter. That the truth is that their souls were there as well, and heard and received the Torah. When they convert, they are merely reconnecting and reclaiming that spiritual heritage that was rightfully theirs from so long ago, where we all accepted the divine mission as one united people.

May our souls re-accept the Torah on a regular basis.

Dedication

To the unifying Sukah of the Lefler family.

BERESHIT   SHEMOT   VAYIKRA   BAMIDBAR   **DEVARIM**   Netziv
Devarim Vaetchanan Ekev Reeh Shoftim Ki Tetze Ki Tavo Nitzavim Vayelech Haazinu
Vezot Habracha

Stolen Inheritance

You may not be able to leave your children a great inheritance, but day by day, you may be weaving coats for them which they will wear for all eternity. -Theodore L. Cuyler

Jewish education starts at the youngest possible age. We start by teaching children verses from the Bible, often with a melody. One of the first verses and perhaps one of the most important ones is from Deuteronomy 33:4:

"The Torah was commanded to us by Moses, an inheritance of the congregation of Jacob."

There is something fundamental about the fact that Moses transmitted the words of God to us. And there is something equally important about the Torah being our inheritance.

The Netziv explains this verse further and states that not only is the Torah, Jewish law and tradition our inheritance, not only is it central to Jewish life and continuity, but whoever withholds the transmission of Jewish jurisprudence from their students is as if they are stealing their inheritance.

Parents have not only the responsibility, but the obligation to pass on the chain of tradition to their children. And if their own parents failed in that transmission, it does not absolve them of reclaiming that treasure and passing it on to future generations. It is woefully true that in many families the chain has been broken. Lip service is paid to our Jewish heritage. The most minimal, superficial, watered-down aspects of Judaism are sometimes all that remains. There is so much more!

Let us not be the generation that let the chain remain broken. Let us reforge the chain. Let us insure a Jewish tomorrow for our families. It starts with education.

Dedication

To Ronit Stolovas and Nadia Dzimalkowski who have taken upon themselves the coordination of meals for the Uruguayan Shabbos Project – the biggest communal education project of the year.

BERESHIT SHEMOT VAYIKRA BAMIDBAR **DEVARIM** Ibn Ezra
Devarim Vaetchanan Ekev Reeh Shoftim Ki Tetze Ki Tavo Nitzavim Vayelech Haazinu Vezot Habracha

Long Live the Constitution

"There is something behind the throne greater than the King himself." - William Pitt The Elder Chatham

Since the beginning of civilization, kings and rulers have been a necessary part of the hierarchical and organizational food chain. Once the community, society or country reaches a certain size and sophistication, there needs to be one person taking charge of the group. For the majority of history, such a person was a King.

However, being American-born and mostly American-educated I have a special affinity and even love for the U.S. constitution. It enshrines and codifies the supremacy of principles over personalities and has mostly averted the excesses that are the norm of despots. There is something greater than the appointed ruler.

Ibn Ezra on Deuteronomy 33:5 makes a related connection. The Torah in the verse speaks of a King, but Ibn Ezra explains that it is really alluding to the Torah itself. Not only the majesty, the nobility, the grandeur, the necessity and the requirement of having, respecting and honoring the Torah, but also the supremacy that Torah should have in our lives. The Torah is the boss, the Torah is the one calling the shots. The Torah, its principles and instructions are the ones we need to follow, more so than any appointed bureaucrat or royal personality.

May we find the kingly principles of the Torah that apply to us and pay them proper homage.

Dedication

To the Torah. May we dance with it in joy (and not drunkenness…)

BERESHIT SHEMOT VAYIKRA BAMIDBAR **DEVARIM**   Ohr Hachayim
Devarim Vaetchanan Ekev Reeh Shoftim Ki Tetze Ki Tavo Nitzavim Vayelech Haazinu
Vezot Habracha

International House of Prayer

"For My house shall be called a house of prayer for all the nations." - Isaiah 56:7

There is much written in the Bible, the Talmud and later Rabbinic literature as to the place of the Jewish people amongst the nations. One of the most direct lines is God's statement that the Jews shall become "a nation of priests" (Kohanim). Many of us are familiar with the term "Kohen" (priest) and the exalted status they have in Jewish history and society. However, what many may have forgotten is that the root of the word, the formative verb, is "lekhahen" (to serve).

Simply put, the nation of Israel is meant to serve the nations of the world. To be a beacon of wisdom, morality, justice and kindness. Not a far off, distant light that gives no warmth, but a close, approachable hearth that welcomes those that wish to warm themselves and learn and share in our experiences. To set an example of families, communities and hopefully a country worth emulating. To assist others in connecting to our positive values and historic lessons.

The Ohr Hachayim (on Deuteronomy 33:7) goes even further in his analysis. Not only is there a need by the nations of the world for the Jewish people, there is a symbiotic and even an eschatologically (look it up...) dependent relationship. Jews need the Gentiles and cannot fulfill their mission without them. The most poignant example, the one that the Ohr Hachayim highlights, is the story of Ruth the Moabite (see my ongoing novelization).

He claims that while the tribe of Judah was destined to produce the king of Israel, that destiny would never come to play until the Gentile, Ruth the Moabite, brought her unique spark to the people of Israel. Only then could Jewish and world history follow its course and lead to a better future.

May we live to see Isaiah's prophecy fulfilled, that the House of God in Jerusalem shall truly be a House of Prayer for all the nations.

Dedication

To my Gentile friends and readers. You are sparks that I'm honored to glean much light from.

בראשית	שמות	ויקרא	במדבר	דברים
נח	וארא	צו	נשא	ואתחנן
לך לך	בא	שמיני	בהעלותך	עקב
וירא	בשלח	תזריע	שלח לך	ראה
חיי שרה	יתרו	מצורע	קרח	שופטים
תולדות	משפטים	אחרי מות	חקת	כי תצא
ויצא	תרומה	קדושים	בלק	כי תבוא
וישלח	תצוה	אמור	פינחס	ניצבים
וישב	כי תשא	בהר	מטות	וילך
מקץ	ויקהל	בחוקותי	מסעי	האזינו
ויגש	פקודי			וזאת הברכה
ויחי				

In Memoriam - Rav Yehuda Amital ZT"L

Rav Amital was many things to many people. I got to know him while in his Yeshiva, as well as for my being the neighbor of one of his daughters. In the Yeshiva, I became an avid fan of his relatively short and succinct words of Torah. He taught much, in powerful, passionate, direct orations. He taught the supreme importance of consistency and diligence in our study and worship. He taught the priority of caring, sensitivity and action over merely text, doctrine and study. He warned of the danger of fanaticism and superficial excitement in ones religiosity. He pushed for more common sense and less mysticism, though he was not afraid to quote from Kabbalistic texts and sources.

But besides his down-to-earth erudition and his practical, clear-headed view of issues, I got to know him on a personal level.

We shared several Shabbat meals together as well as Pesach Seders and family celebrations. And that is where I got to see the family man. The husband, father, grandfather and great-grandfather delighting in each person of his large and blessed family.

Over the years, I had the opportunity to consult with him on personal matters. He always took the time and had the interest to hear me out, to understand the essence of the issue and provide much needed guidance. What impressed me most, besides his wisdom, was the care and responsibility he was willing to take in assisting me with my concerns.

Through his life, he was a guide and an inspiration to thousands upon thousands of people. I was fortunate to have been one of them.

Thanks!

This has been very much a family effort; especially having my mother proofread every single *dvar tora* for the past eight years, my wife who would censor some of my more inflammatory ones, and my father-in-law who designed this gorgeous book cover as well as all the covers of my other books.

I am of course indebted to the many teachers, Rabbis and role models who have given me the encouragement and guidance in my Torah studies.

But most keenly, I am thankful to the many, many readers over the years that thanked me, commented and even criticized my *dvar tora*s. It gives an author tremendous pleasure as well as continued motivation to know that his words are being read.

And ultimately, God, who has given me this capacity to spread some of His Torah.

About the Author

Ben-Tzion Spitz is a prolific writer of biblical and rabbinic themes. Much of his writing can be found on his blog at ben-tzion.com, where he has published dozens of biblical fiction stories, three biblical fiction novels, and biblical analysis based on ancient, medieval and contemporary sources. He has been exploring and researching biblical stories and archeological findings for over two decades.

He generally lives in Alon Shvut, Israel, with his wife and their seven children. He is currently in Montevideo on assignment as Chief Rabbi of Uruguay.

Made in the USA
Charleston, SC
02 January 2016